APPLIED MODERN COMBATIVES

A Rising Phoenix Martial Arts Student Handbook

By Tom Gillis

Applied Modern Combatives
Student Resource Book

Tom Gillis

Tom Gillis

2015

Copyright © 2015 by FTS Inc.

All rights reserved. This book or any portion thereof may not be reproduced or used in any manner whatsoever without the express written permission of the publisher except for the use of brief quotations in a book review or scholarly journal.

First Printing: 2015

ISBN 978-0-9939421-1-2

FTS Inc.
118 Cimarron Grove Road
Okotoks Alberta Canada T1S 2H1

www.ftsma.com

Ordering Information:

Special discounts are available on quantity purchases by corporations, associations, educators, and others. For details, contact the publisher at the above listed address.

U.S. trade bookstores and wholesalers: Please contact FTS Inc. Tel: (403) 829-7897or email info@ftsma.com

Dedication

To all my students past, present, and future. Stay safe and be well.

Table of Contents

Introduction	9
Training Methodology and Tactical Priorities	11
Interpersonal Communication	17
Use of Force	21
Strikes	26
Inside Position Combatives	29
Takedowns	33
Ground Fighting	37
Edged Weapon Defense	45
First Aid Self Aid	48
Crime Prevention	50

Introduction

Thank you for choosing to train in the Reality Based Training Program. This program was originally created for members of the law enforcement community. As it gained momentum however it increasingly became popular among non-law enforcement and particularly women. This is mainly due to the focus of the program.

The class is 24 hours in length and only covers approximately 14 techniques. The movements are easy to learn and, as seen in Chapter 1, based on tactics and natural body movement. This makes it easy for beginners to pick up the material quickly and because there are few techniques there's a lot of time to practice them in a variety of situations and under increased stress. This leads to a deeper understanding of the material and a higher retention of the information.

The program, or its individual modules and chapters, have been delivered to dozens of police agencies around the world and hundreds of civilians. The material has been used in actual situations with great success to the point where authorized instructors in the police community have passed it on to firefighters and emergency medical personnel with great success.

I hope you enjoy the class and this training aid which will help you through the program.

Tom Gillis

> **Training Methodology and Tactical Priorities**
>
> *It is crucial that before learning physical techniques participants have a firm understanding on the 6 Tactical Priorities during an incident and how to care for themselves after an incident. These are fundamentals that participants will be encouraged to develop during their skill development and continue to practice once operational.*

Chapter Testing Objectives

1. Explain the Training Methodology
2. List and describe the 6 Tactical Priorities during contact with subjects
3. List and describe 3 considerations for action after a critical incident
4. Demonstrate a basic understanding of Post Traumatic Stress Disorder

Training Methodology

This program views training physical skills for students slightly differently than most other service providers. As you can see by the graphic below Physical Techniques ARE NOT the most important priority.

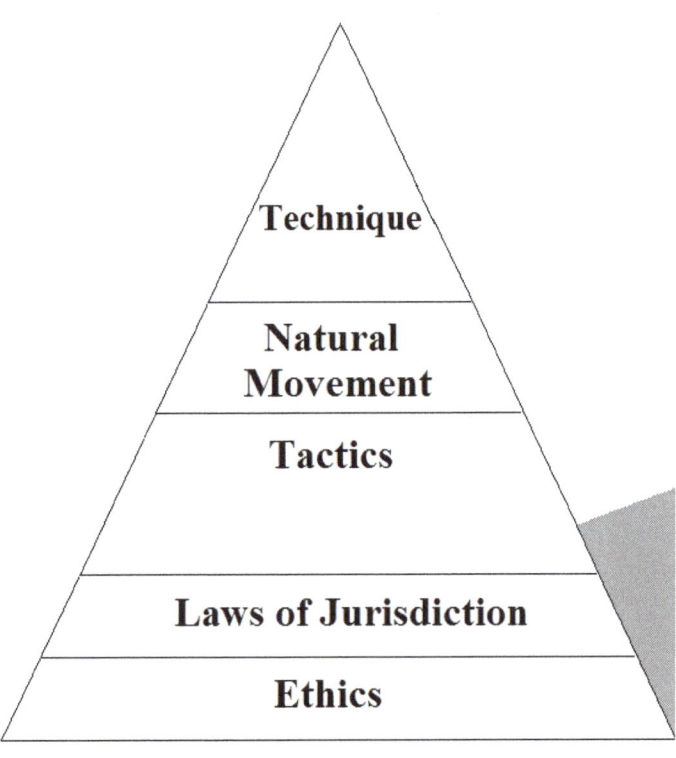

Ethics

As illustrated above the foundation for all training is Ethical Behavior. We maintain that the protection of life is the top priority. Ethical behavior means knowing AND doing what's right to protect life. This includes your life, the lives of any bystanders, and to do what they can to protect the Subject(s) even in combative situations and definitely post conflict when you're safe. This means that at no time is it acceptable for you to take any actions that unnecessarily cause harm to any person. This means taking unnecessary risks (i.e. speeding unnecessarily) are not acceptable, and the onus is on you to train your skills to be able to protect life at all times.

This type of training goes beyond just training schema for the typical perceived stimulus: react paradigm and focus' on being present in all situations and making conscious decisions based on the totality of circumstances. There are many documented cases of people who received this type of training making reasonable mistakes in situations that have caused serious injury and in some circumstances unnecessary death (i.e. BART weapon confusion case). Instead the goal of training should be to instill a sense of presence in situations which encourages students to process the environment and make rapid conscious decisions. This level of proficiency takes a lot of work to reach but with hard work and dedication it is possible.

Law

Citizens have a duty to lead by example by following the laws, rules, regulations, and policies in effect. The focus should be on Reasonable and Necessary Use of Force. Remember however that the law cannot violate Ethical Behavior. You must understand any statutory and case laws in effect in your jurisdiction.

This means that there is an onus on trainers to research, know, and understand the law and be able to transmit it accurately to students. This level of understanding goes far beyond typical Use of Force Models (which aren't law but rather visual representations of law).

For example recent case law indicates that trainers have a responsibility to train officers in their charge in all weapons, at all ranges.

Tactics

Combatives training should teach students Tactics that are applicable to a variety of situations.

Some examples include (but aren't limited to);

- Shielding and cornering
- Angular Movement
- Changing elevation
- Jamming opponents attacks before they have time to initiate
- Controlling space
- Engagement and disengagement
- 5 point balance manipulation

Natural Movement

Any physical material taught in a class must follow rules of Natural Movement. This means it is imperative that instructors are constantly evaluating material and asking if what they're teaching violates these rules.

The Rules for Natural Movement are;

Limbs are Springs. The legs are responsible for lifting, and moving and work best when they have a slight flex in them. The knees should never be locked while moving. When punching the elbow should maintain a slight flex. Locking out the joints effects the bodies ability to move well and can cause hyperextension injury.

Balance. Maintain balance by keeping the head over the hips and back straight. Keeping your eyes up and alert to your surroundings will help to keep a straight back.

Respect your Center Line. Limbs don't cross your own center line, and if they do correct it immediately. This means that while moving your feet should never be crossed. When moving left the left leg should move first by pushing off the ground with the right and vice versa.

Joint Stability. The less a joint moves the more stable it is. One way to tell the natural position of a joint is to stand relaxed with your arms loosely at your sides and examine the way the joints align. While moving they should maintain this alignment. For example many people twist their wrist while punching so that the hand is horizontal to the ground. If you stand naturally and lift your arm you'll notice that your hand is vertical (thumb points up) for example.

Arms push and legs pull. By understanding the most powerful and efficient use of the body you can maximize power and strength generation.

> *To learn what this rule means try this exercise;*
>
> *With a partner grab their wrist and step back away from them extending your arm. Try to pull them towards you with just your arm and have them resist slightly. Now repeat the exercise but this time start close to your partner and hold your elbow to your core. Now step back and pull them with your legs. Notice a difference?*
>
> *Now stand back from your partner and extend your arms and put your hands on their chest. Have your partner resist as you push with your legs. To learn how to push properly stand closer to your partner and put your hands on their chest with your elbows close to your core. Keep your feet firmly planted on the ground and push with your arms by extending forwards with your elbows.*

The Head is the Bodies Steering Wheel. Where the head leads the body will follow. One of the most efficient ways to know where someone's body will go is to know where their eyes are looking. This means that to maintain an upright stable posture your own eyes should be up and aware of your surroundings. Not looking at the ground. This also means that if you can direct an opponents vision in a particular direction you can manipulate their balance in that direction.

Technique

When Tactics are combined with Natural Movement in a manner that is Ethical, Legal Techniques are created. Techniques CANNOT violate any of the previous levels of development. Techniques that promote the students self discovery and promote a sense of balance, co-ordination, timing, precision, and power are best. A training regime in which techniques build on each other are more desirable than a training program where each technique is different.

When teaching techniques the goal is to teach the student to the point where it exists in the brain stem, and not the pre frontal lobe. Sports science research indicates that an effective way to do this is to limit the amount of time they can work on a piece of material to approximately 20 minutes, take a break from that material, and then come back to it within an hour.

Tactical Priorities

There are 6 tactical priorities that, in conjunction with physical skills, can increase safety in a violent altercation. In fact in some instances it's the application of these priorities in conjunction within the guidelines of Reasonable Force that will allow you to decide which tactics or techniques to use. Most people that are attacked and injured are attacked because they gave the subject the opportunity to hurt them. By using these fundamentals in every contact with assailants you can effectively eliminate some this opportunity.

The Tactical Priorities are;

Priority #1, Don't get hit.

Unlike in a combat sport competition, your first priority during any contact with an assailant should be to not get struck by that person. During street altercations there are no rules, no safety equipment, and often no one to help if you get hurt. Assailants can deploy weapons and even in the case of an empty hand altercation you can't be sure of a subjects intent or if and when they'll stop attacking. For this reason the first priority is to not get hit. The first hit in a street altercation might be the last. There are several tactics that you can use to maximize their chances of not getting hit;

- **Cover, concealment, and shielding.** Understanding the differences between cover, concealment, and shielding and using them effectively can greatly increase your safety. Cover is something that will stop the threat from penetrating. It is accepted that something that will stop a bullet is cover. Concealment will allow you to hide yourself from the assailant but will not stop weapons from penetrating through. A car door in a gun fight is concealment. In situations where cover isn't available use items for shielding, such as chairs, tables, and wall corners. Shields provide an obstacle that a subject must navigate to reach you but won't stop weapons and doesn't effectively block line of sight. By using shielding you can effectively slow down an attacker.

- **Move on 45, stay alive.** The use of angular movement can move you out of the way of incoming attacks and cause the subject to recalculate where you are and how to continue an attack. Using 45 degree angular movement relative to a subject can also open opportunities for counter attacks and control techniques.

- **Pre-attack Indicators.** Often assailants who attack people display some threat cues just before the attack. An observant person will pick up on these threat cues and be prepared to take action. Some pre-attack indicators include;

    - Verbal cues such as pitch, tone, volume, rate, and language used including profanity and threats.

- Facial cues include pupil dilation, protruding eyes, nervous eye movement, squinting, furrowed brow, clenched jaw, eye movement which includes looking around for witnesses, targets, or escape route, and the thousand yard stare.

- Postural movements might include clenched fists, indexing a location on the body or environment, shifting the feet, closing the range, and cutting you off from a possible escape route.

- **Maintain Distance.** Reaction time is defined as the amount of time between when something is observed, processed, a plan formulated, and motor neurons begin to initiate a motor response. You can increase the amount of time they have to complete this process by increasing the distance to a threat. The further the distance from an assailant the more time you'll have to react to their actions. This relationship can work against you too. If there is too much space from the subject they will have more time to react when physical control is attempted. The minimum distance maintained to a subject should be no less than a step and an arm's reach and greater depending on the situation.

- **Watch for Multiples.** Often time's people find themselves faced with multiple opponents or opponents with multiple weapons. This of course can be dangerous especially when the defender deals with the initial threat and then lowers their guard. For this reason it is important to remember that once a threat is recognized and neutralized to continue to look for others.

- **Keep your hands up.** Always during contact with a subject(s) you should remember to keep your hands up. An easy way to remember this is to index your belt or waistline or talk with your hands. If the assailants actions become somewhat escalated the hands can be raised and used for non-verbal communication at chest or chin level. If an assaultive altercation happens the hands should stay up at face level.

- **De-escalate when available.** The use of calm verbal communication can effectively de-escalate a situation and decrease your chance of injury. Remember to maintain your calm control and strive to deescalate situations before they become aggressive. Subjects may try to goad you into an altercation by being rude and disrespectful.

- **Disengagement.** Disengagement is a consideration that you may employ in an attempt to control a situation. If you cannot safely control a situation, or if disengagement would assist in controlling a situation with a lower level of force, you should disengage from the incident. Disengagement may not be possible in some circumstances. Environmental factors such as obstacles or barriers may physically prevent you leaving. As well, the distance between you and the assailant, and the weapon being used by the assailant may also eliminate the use of this option. Lastly, the safety of your family or others around you may dictate that disengagement is not an option.

Tactical Priority #2, Hit Back.

Hit Back means that you employ techniques to take the initiative and put an assailant on the reaction side of the situation. Often times however you won't know you're under attack until after it starts. Once you've determined that an attack is imminent and what actions are reasonable you can initiate techniques towards the assailant.

Tactical Priority #3, Finish the Fight.

Finish the Fight can change in any given situation given the totality of the circumstances and it might just be because the assailant has lost the intent to fight, perhaps the subject is unconscious or deceased in the case of an application of lethal force. You must make a commitment before an altercation to never give up. Every confrontation is <u>winnable</u>. If something isn't working change tactics and continue on. Developing a winning mentality also includes preparing before you head out, maintaining a high degree of physical fitness, and using imagery and visualization.

> *It should be noted here that in some instances priorities 1-3 happen simultaneously. For instance if a subject were to produce a knife and lunge at you and you move out of the way, produces your own knife and engage with lethal force cutting the subject and the cut stops the assailant than in that case priorities 1-3 happened together.*
>
> *However the situation unfolds once the assailants unable or unwilling to continue to engage in their assaultive behavior you must continue on to the second part of the priority list. It should be noted that depending on the situation priorities 4-6 might change order. They are provided below in a general format that will fit most situations;*

Tactical Priority #4, Escape and Evade.

At this stage of an altercation get to safety!

Tactical Priority #5, Call for help.

Depending on the lethality of the situation you might swap priority 4 and 5. If for instance if you or someone else are injured getting Emergency Services on the way might be more important. In the case of injuries the amount of time from when the injury occurred to when treatment begins can make the difference between life and death. For this reason it's recommended that as soon as possible you should call for help. In the best case scenario this would be before an altercation even began. If however you find yourself surprised that may be impossible.

Tactical Priority #6, Self aid/first aid.

As soon as safe to do so check yourself for injuries and then other people. Although you might want to help other people first it is impossible for you to treat someone effectively and ongoing if you're too wounded to help them.

For this reason give yourself a primary survey to assess the extent of your injuries first and then decide if you need to treat yourself or others first.

Conclusion

During a violent situation following the 6 Tactical Priorities can help you make good decisions and maximize your safety. The 6 Tactical Priorities are Don't Get Hit, Hit Back, Finish the Fight, Escape and Evade, 1st Aid/Self Aid, Call for Help. Depending on the totality of circumstances the priorities might change order. This framework, along with an understanding of Reasonable Force, can be used to dictate your actions.

> ## *Interpersonal Communication*
>
> *Communication Skills are possibly the most difficult to develop and should continually be worked on. Poor communication can lead to physical violence whereas excellent communication skills can often de-escalate a situation and resolve conflict before it becomes physical.*
>
> *Because every situation is different a single script or dialogue cannot be followed. Instead our method is to understand why people communicate in certain ways and understand how to apply certain principles and concepts to a situation to increase the chance of a non violent outcome. This method allows officers to operate in ways that are comfortable for them and allows for change during rapidly evolving situations.*

Chapter Testing Objectives

1. Describe why communication breaks down between people.
2. Describe and demonstrate methods for building rapport and de-escalate verbal conflict.

Understanding why communication breaks down.

Generally speaking people see themselves as intellectual animals capable of reason and logic under all circumstances. This belief however is an illusion. People are emotional animals who use intellect. It is important to understand this difference because during confrontational situations emotion rather than intellect takes over. This is why some people "just don't get it" or can't understand that they're being unreasonable or even dangerous.

Basic communication model

In any verbal conflict there are 3 main components at play. The situation will take form depending on how these components interact. The components are;

- a) What the transmitter thinks they're transmitting
- b) The actual message being transmitted
- c) What the receiver thinks they're receiving

Factors that influence the relationship between these 3 factors are;

- Language barriers of the parties
- Ethnicity
- Religion
- Gender
- State of mind
- Subject matter
- Level of education
- Level of buy-in to the situation

Often what happens is the actual message isn't what either party perceives it to be. The transmitter thinks that they are sending a certain message but the words they're using, the tone and pitch of their voice, and their non-verbal communications are not what they perceive them to be.

Likewise due to the receivers' personal circumstances the message gets interpreted upon being received. The receiver interprets the message based on their own circumstances and assigns value to it.

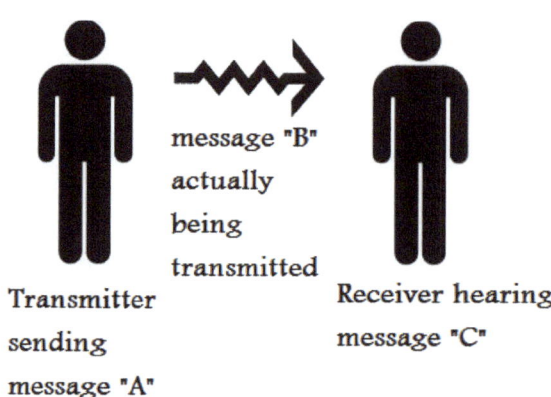

The net result is that neither party are getting what they require in the situation. This cycle can continue back and forth between two unskilled communicators. As the cycle continues emotions increase and even less of the message(s) are received as they were intended.

Due to increased emotions and stress this situation will result in 1 of 2 possible outcomes unless the cycle is broken;

Fight

Both parties become so emotional and frustrated that a physical confrontation ensues between them. This increases chance of injury to both the officer and the subject and the public and increases likelihood of property damage.

Flight

One or both parties become so frustrated by the in ability to resolve the issue that they completely shut down and leave the situation. In this case the officer may now be forced into a flight situation or have to initiate physical contact to restrain the subject.

Breaking the cycle

Once this negative communication cycle is understood you can begin to interrupt the cycle at various points to increase the likelihood that communication skills will resolve the situation. Before this can be attempted however a few important points must be remembered. They are;

- Communication skills are as important as physical skills
- Be patient
- Recognize when to switch from communication skills to physical skills
- Evaluate the extent of risk of injury to bystanders, yourself, and the other person as well as risk of property damage when deciding to continue communication skills or switch to physical skills.

Likewise there are communication traps that should be avoided. They are;

- Promising things you're not 100% sure you can deliver
- Threatening action that you're not 100% willing to follow up on
- Using phrases such as "calm down", "relax", "I know what you're going through."
- Raising voice, putting hands on hips, crossing arms, not looking at subject, glaring at subject, smirking, inappropriate laughter, and other non verbal communications that are disrespectful will create barriers to communication

Breaking the cycle step 1. Create rapport

Rapport is the feeling of being connected between two parties. This is essential in communicating with subjects. People want to feel they're being heard and listened to. The following steps will help officers to build rapport;

- Use positive language and encourage "yes questions". This is accomplished by asking a question that you already know the answer to be yes. An example may be "the property owner asked you to leave and you don't feel that's fair yes?"

- Maintain distance. People are defensive when they feel their personal space is being violated. A reactionary space of approximately a step and an arm's reach should be maintained at all times.

- Don't stand directly in front of the subject. Not only is this not tactically sound but it also sends a confrontational message. Whenever possible walk in the same direction of a subject off to the side as you're communicating with them. If you can't do that then step just off to one side or the other while still in front of them.

- As soon as you notice the subject repeating the same phrase or message over and again recognize that they're trapped in a cycle where they don't feel you've heard them. Paraphrase their message back to them and ask them if you got it correct.

- Always keep in mind that this might be a new situation for the subject and they're likely confused and stressed about it. Ask yourself how you'd want to be treated in their shoes.

- Know your facts. Don't assume anything.

- Keep your voice loud and firm but not yelling or rude. Maintain sound tactical body posture. Keep your hands up in front of your chest talking with your hands. Keep moving slightly from side to side or back and forth. This all indicates to a would-be combative person that you're relaxed but ready for escalation. This show of force may deter them from initiating a fight.

Breaking the cycle step 2. Making your sales pitch.

Once rapport is obtained you should change your focus on to moving forwards with the purpose of obtaining the other persons involvement. Reinforce that you're interested in a peaceful resolution. If they don't respond positively remind them that fighting will only make the situation worse for everyone involved.

- Remind them that you're not criticising them or who they are but rather you're only interest is to resolve the situation.

- Use please and thank and show compassion and respect.

- Try to use the "Law of Reciprocity." This is a human communication law that transcends culture, ethnicity, and religious barriers. The Law of Reciprocity means that if you can make the other person feel indebted to you they are more likely to pay that debt with positive behavior. This is a powerful tactic used in sales and has saved large corporations from going bankrupt when used on a large scale.

- If the other party escalates their behavior by raising their voice, using profanity, indexing common places for weapons, begins looking around nervously, cutting you off from an exit route, suddenly goes quiet and stares "through" you, or constantly attempts to decrease distance and keep you directly in front of them, it's time to prepare for physical violence. Depending on the situation, if a combination of these factors are present the best plan is for you to initiate the physical confrontation.

> *Use of Force*
>
> *It is crucial that participants thoroughly understand what Canadian law is surrounding the Use Of Force. It is critical that each participant be able to understand the appropriate sections of the criminal code and have a working understanding of the underlying principles in the sections regulating use of force.*
>
> *This section is not intended to substitute legal studies but rather to be used as an introduction and to help participants understand the framework what's legal to do to protect themselves during an assault.*

Chapter Testing Objectives

1. At the end of this session each participant will be able to:
2. Explain section 34 of the Canadian Criminal Code
3. Explain what is meant by "Totality of Circumstances"
4. Explain consequences of excessive force

Use of Force

The Canadian Criminal Code (CCC) contains guidelines for Private Citizens for using force against another person in Self Defense.

Instead of trying to fit these laws and their underlying principles into a visual model, which would be limiting in its application, you should instead thoroughly understand what the laws are and how to apply them and critically think in stressful circumstances. This is achieved by first understanding what the law says, then reviewing its application through case studies, then applying this understanding in theoretical table top studies, and then applying this understanding in physical practice.

Defence — use or threat of force

☐ **34.** (1) A person is not guilty of an offence if

- (*a*) they believe on reasonable grounds that force is being used against them or another person or that a threat of force is being made against them or another person;

- (*b*) the act that constitutes the offence is committed for the purpose of defending or protecting themselves or the other person from that use or threat of force; and

- (*c*) the act committed is reasonable in the circumstances.

(2) In determining whether the act committed is reasonable in the circumstances, the court shall consider the relevant circumstances of the person, the other parties and the act, including, but not limited to, the following factors:

- (*a*) the nature of the force or threat;

- (*b*) the extent to which the use of force was imminent and whether there were other means available to respond to the potential use of force;

- (*c*) the person's role in the incident;

- (*d*) whether any party to the incident used or threatened to use a weapon;

- (*e*) the size, age, gender and physical capabilities of the parties to the incident;

- (*f*) the nature, duration and history of any relationship between the parties to the incident, including any prior use or threat of force and the nature of that force or threat;

- (*f.1*) any history of interaction or communication between the parties to the incident;

- (*g*) the nature and proportionality of the person's response to the use or threat of force; and

- (*h*) whether the act committed was in response to a use or threat of force that the person knew was lawful.

(3) Subsection (1) does not apply if the force is used or threatened by another person for the purpose of doing something that they are required or authorized by law to do in the administration or enforcement of the law, unless the person who commits the act that constitutes the offence believes on reasonable grounds that the other person is acting unlawfully.

What this means is that if you use force to protect yourself, you MAY BE entitled to the legal defense of Self Defense to the assault you just committed on the other party. In order to be found not guilty of that assault the judge is going to look at the total set of circumstances and determine if your actions were REASONABLE and NECESSARY given the circumstances.

The totality of circumstances can be defined as the relationship that exists between both parties and the circumstances that brought them together.

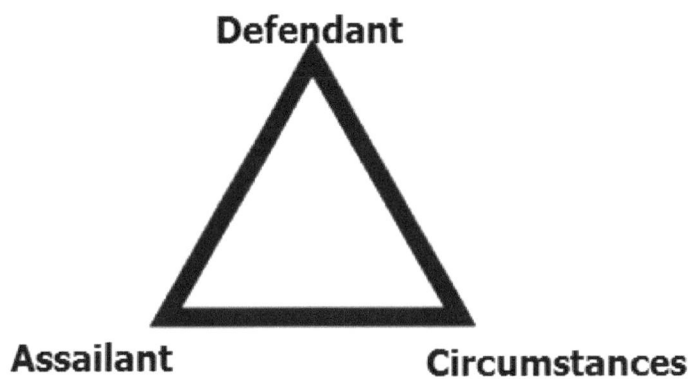

1. Defendant Variables.

There are several variables that you bring into the situation that will determine what force is reasonable for that situation. They include, but aren't limited to;

- Height, weight, build
- Fitness level
- Hydration and nutrition
- Exhaustion
- Skill set
- Confidence level
- Equipment
- Availability of help
- Number of people helping you

2. Assailant Variables.

There are several variables that an assailant(s) bring into the situation that will determine what force is reasonable for that situation. These factors are always in relation to your Factors. They include, but aren't limited to;

- Height, weight, build
- Observable fitness level indicators
- Observable skill set indicators
- Observable confidence level indicators
- Observable indicators of mental health concerns or intoxication
- Observable indicators or subjects willingness to co-operate
- Weapons
- Number of subjects present at scene

3. Circumstantial Variables.

There are several variables that circumstance(s) during a situation that will determine what force is reasonable for that situation. These factors are always in relation to you and your assailants Factors. They include, but aren't limited to;

- Original reason the parties having contact with each other
- Seriousness of any offences being committed
- Environmental variables (light, weather, footing, environmental dangers, environmental weapons)
- Availability of escape for both parties
- Availability of Shielding, Cover, and Concealment
- Known history or intelligence surrounding the Subject or the situation
- your ability to maintain distance to the assailant(s)

Totality of Circumstances

The term totality of circumstances therefore can be thought of as the relationship between the Defendant (D), the Assailant (A), and the Circumstances(C). This relationship can be visually represented as

$$D+A+C = \text{Reasonable Force}$$

This process must be completed very quickly and be ongoing. As a situation unfolds this relationship will continue to change. Research indicates that these changes can happen as quickly as 1:100th of a second. This means that you must continually be asking yourself what the reasonable options are during a situation or a confrontation.

Consequences of Excessive Force

Whether through negligence or on purpose people who are found to have used excessive force during a situation or confrontation may be faced with the following repercussions;

- Criminal charges/conviction
- Civil liabilities from victims, families, or employers

Section 27

Use of force to prevent commission of offence

27. Every one is justified in using as much force as is reasonably necessary

(a) to prevent the commission of an offence

(i) for which, if it were committed, the person who committed it might be arrested without warrant, and

(ii) that would be likely to cause immediate and serious injury to the person or property of anyone; or

(b) to prevent anything being done that, on reasonable grounds, he believes would, if it were done, be an offence mentioned in paragraph (a).

R.S., c. C-34, s. 27.

Discussion

You may use force to prevent Criminal Offences. Some examples to use are;

- A subject is about to break into a property but hasn't completed the offence yet
- A subject is about to vandalize a property but hasn't completed the offence yet
- A subject is about to assault someone but you're not sure if it meets the Imminent requirement

Conclusion

During a combat situation you are responsible for your decisions and actions. You are allowed to use force but the Canadian Criminal Code and Case law have defined what that force can be. Section 34 of the Canadian Criminal Code defines your force options as Reasonable, and cannot be Excessive.

To define which options in a tactical scenario are Reasonable and which are Excessive you must take into account the Totality of Circumstances.

If a court finds that you used excessive force, you may find themselves subject to criminal conviction and penalty.

> ### *Strikes*
>
> *There has been, and continues to be much controversy surrounding the idea of striking an adversary. It is thought that public perception looks unfavorably upon strikes because it appears like they're delivered out of anger, frustration, and panic.*
>
> *This is not the intended motivation behind striking another person however. Rather strikes are used for two primary reasons. First they distract the adversary from staying strong in their structure and joints opening a window for follow up skeletal control, and second they give you an entry into establishing position and posture from which you can deploy follow up control methods.*

Chapter Testing Objectives

1. Explain the motivation behind striking someone.
2. Demonstrate the Straight Punch.
3. Demonstrate the Palm Heel Strike.
4. Demonstrate the 3 Elbow Strikes.
5. Demonstrate the Knee Strike.

Understanding Strikes

Contrary to popular belief, strikes are an unreliable method of controlling someone. This is for a variety of reasons. First strikes to control someone primarily rely on a pain response. Because people have a wide spectrum of responses to pain it's unknown how anyone will respond. Secondly striking applies kinetic energy and then cycles off the target thereby not actually controlling anything or limiting someone's ability to continue to move.

In use of force cases from around the world subjects continue to assault their victims even after receiving multiple strikes. A goal orientated attacker can ignore the pain caused by being struck and continue their violent and illegal action.

For these reasons strikes may not cause any type of impairment in an adversary's ability to move their body or use their skeletal muscle. The majority of people who cease their assaultive action due to striking do it because they either choose to because of the pain of the strikes or because they're rendered unconscious.

Understanding how to strike is beneficial for two reasons however.

First it can provide a defender the opportunity to regain their structure and position in a fight. Most attacks are a surprise attack. This often puts the would be victim behind in terms of reaction time and most often results in them moving rewards. A strike by its very nature moves forwards. For this reason strikes are an effective means of moving forwards again and reestablishing skeletal posture and maintaining balance as well as possibly offsetting the physical and mental balance of the attacker.

Secondly striking can create entry points to make the necessary attachments for follow up methods of skeletal control. Striking often allows a window of opportunity for follow up control methods because the subject, at least for a brief time, is distracted by the strike.

In a best case scenario after receiving a strike a subject will decide to cease their violent illegal action and stop resisting and fighting.

Technique 1. Straight Punch

- The straight punch is the primary strike. It is applied with the striking foot forwards and with a vertical fist. The primary target is an assailant's face.

- To begin step forwards and raise the hands to the chest.

- Once the feet have stopped moving thrust the hand forwards maintaining a vertical fist while simultaneously dropping the center of gravity and slightly rotating the upper body from hips to shoulders and keeping the other hand elevated to protect the upper body and face.

- Make contact with a straight wrist and the flat of the fingers and knuckles.

- Push through the target and once the end of the strike is reached cycle the hand back in a straight line to the body.

Technique #2. Palm Heel Strike

- The primary targets for the Palm Heel Strike are the subjects' upper chest or face. It is an excellent tool for knocking people back and gaining space. It is applied with the striking foot forwards (regardless of where weapons are worn).

- The delivery of the strike starts the same as the Straight Punch. To begin step forwards and raise the hands to the chest.

- Once the feet have stopped moving thrust the hand forwards. Open the fingers and pull them up and back so that they're pointing at the ceiling. Simultaneously drop the center of gravity and slightly rotating the upper body from hips to shoulders and keeping the other hand elevated to protect the upper body and face. Make contact with the base of the hand (the heel of the palm).

- Push through the target and once the end of the strike is reached cycle the hand back in a straight line to the body.

Technique #3. Hammer Fist

- The primary targets for the Hammer Fist are the subjects face or side of their head. It is primarily a close quarters strike and is primarily used when manipulating a subject's skeleton with the other hand.

- To begin the strike step forwards and raise the arms to the chest in a crossed fashion with the forward arm matching the forward leg and elbows bent.

- To deliver the strike rotate into the target and extend the elbow while dropping the center of gravity and closing the fist tightly while turning it so it's horizontal to the ground.

- Contact is made with the meaty portion of the hand under the pinky finger.

Technique #4. Elbow Strikes

- There are many different ways to utilize elbow Strikes. The 4 different Elbow Strikes are all delivered at close quarters. They are the Outside Horizontal Elbow, the Inside Horizontal Elbow, the Uppercut Vertical Elbow, and the Rear Horizontal Elbow. Targeting is to the subjects head.

- All 4 delivery methods utilize some common concepts. They are body rotation, dropping center of gravity at time of impact, forward foot – forward weapon, and impact with the tip of the elbow.

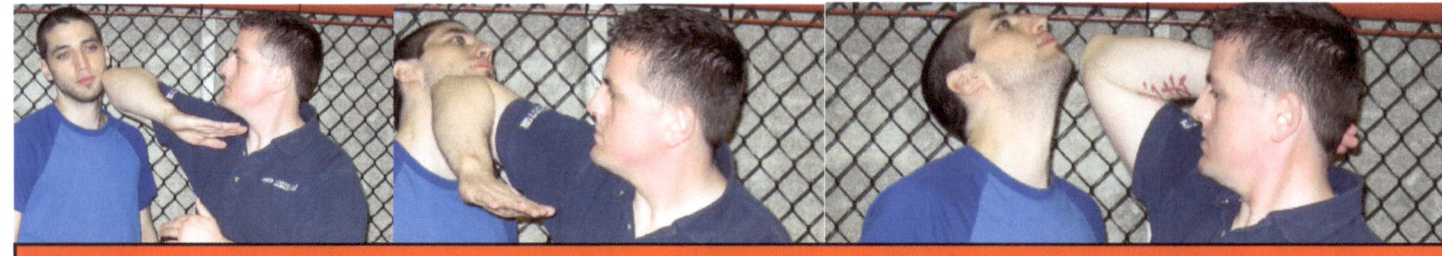

- To deliver an Outside Horizontal Elbow step forwards and raise the corresponding arm, bent in at the elbow so the hand is touching the chest. Rotate the upper body from the hips through the shoulders while simultaneously dropping the center of gravity. Impact is made with the tip of the elbow and a follow through while balance is maintained.

- To deliver an Inside Horizontal Elbow, begin where the Outside Horizontal Elbow finished. Lean forwards into the target while thrusting the elbow forwards into the target.

- To deliver a Uppercut Vertical Elbow begin once again by stepping forwards but this time tuck a vertical arm against the rib cage with a bend at the elbow so that the hand is touching the chest. Begin to lift the elbow through the shoulder while simultaneously lifting up onto the ball of the foot and rotating the hips. The primary target is under the subjects chin. Follow through by pointing the elbow straight to the sky.

- To deliver a Rear Horizontal Elbow start by lifting the hands to the chest with elbows bent. Step rearwards with the foot that corresponds with the elbow you wish to strike with. Lift the elbow so that it's horizontal and rotate through the hips and shoulders while dropping the center of gravity. Impact is made with the tip of the elbow.

Technique #5. Knee Strikes

- Knee strikes are primarily used to strike a subjects legs to temporarily alter their base and structure. After a knee strike immediate skeletal manipulation and follow up control should be used.

- To deploy a Knee Strike first ensure a grip with the hands somewhere on the subjects' arms or bodies.

- Next chamber the leg intended to apply the strike by stretching it rearwards.

- Deliver the strike by pulling the subject into it using the hands and thrust the tip of the knee through the intended target.

- The most effective target zones are the upper legs.

- Immediately after delivering the strike follow up with a control technique or takedown.

Conclusion

While applying strikes to someone can be beneficial to alter their mental or physical balance, strikes shouldn't be relied on to end a confrontation due to the spectrum of pain tolerance and the unreliability and unpredictability of the effectiveness of the strike.

Strikes should never be delivered out of frustration or retribution but rather should only be applied as part of an overall strategy to manipulate the assailants' skeleton and open a window of opportunity for follow up control.

Inside Position Combatives

In combatives the Inside Position is often taught as a position to avoid. Instead outside positions, often referred to as level II ½, and sought and taught to be more desirable. While an outside position does have certain tactical advantages it also poses 2 problems. The first is how do you get to the outside when an opponent is actively assaulting you? In some instances if you are too focused on seeking the outside position you may be prolonging your exposure to the assault instead of fighting back and ending the encounter. The second problem with the outside position during an assault is that it limits your ability to strike targets which may allow more expedient control of the assailant and an end to the assault.

Chapter Testing Objectives

1. Demonstrate the Leg Reap Takedown.
2. Demonstrate the Windmill Takedown.

Understanding the Inside Position.

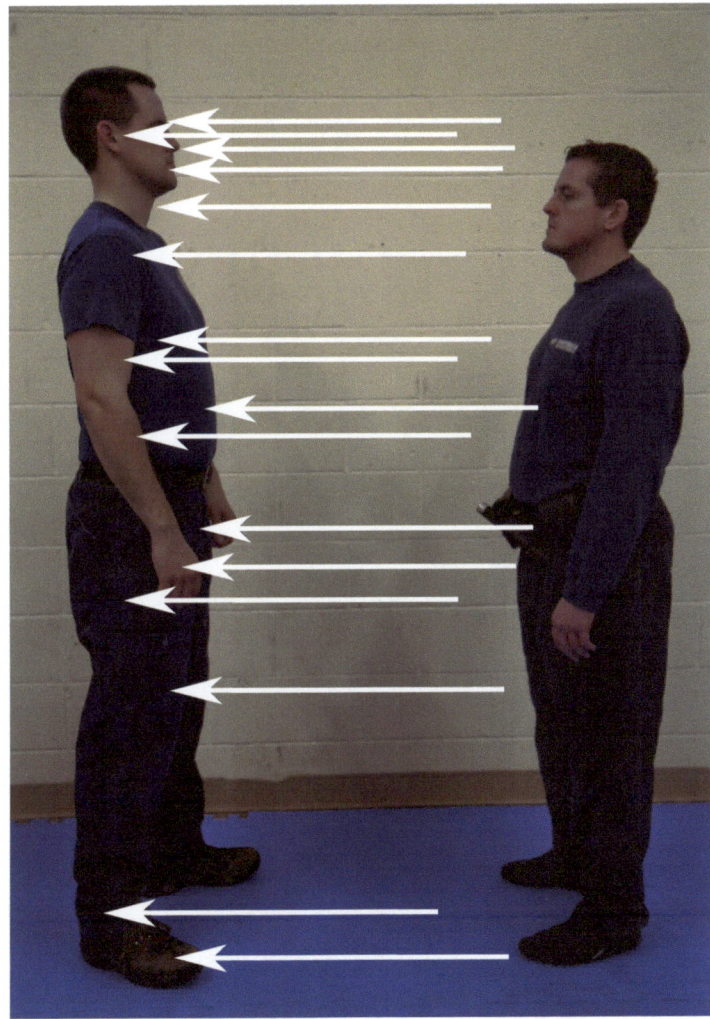

The inside position is defined as, "the position that you occupy, relative to an assailant, that is within a step and arms reach and directly in front of the assailant."

This position is often thought to be dangerous because the subject can attack with hands, feet, knees, elbows, spitting, biting, and head butting (highlighted in white). What's often forgotten however is that you have the same weapon delivery systems available to you (highlighted in white), with the exception of spitting and biting which is only appropriate in very extreme lethal force circumstances.

While an outside position offers protection from an assailants weapon delivery systems and allows you to use yours it also limits the targets available AND can be almost impossible to get to in a real life altercation. An assailant will naturally attempt to keep their target directly in front of them to attack them with these weapon delivery systems.

It's important to keep in mind that an assailants most desirable and incapacitating targets are available from the inside position. Each arrow in figure 2 represents one of the following targets; eyes, nose, ears, mouth, side of the neck, wind pipe/throat, shoulder, bicep, elbow, forearm, wrist/hand/fingers, floating ribs, solar plexus, groin, thigh (inside & outside), knee, shin, ankle, and foot. As you can see with training and practice you can control this position can develop the skill to be quite effective at controlling an assaultive subject in varying degrees of violence and danger.

Inside Position Combatives

Technique 1. Stopping the Initial Strike

- As the assailant attacks with a hook punch step into the attack and raise both arms.

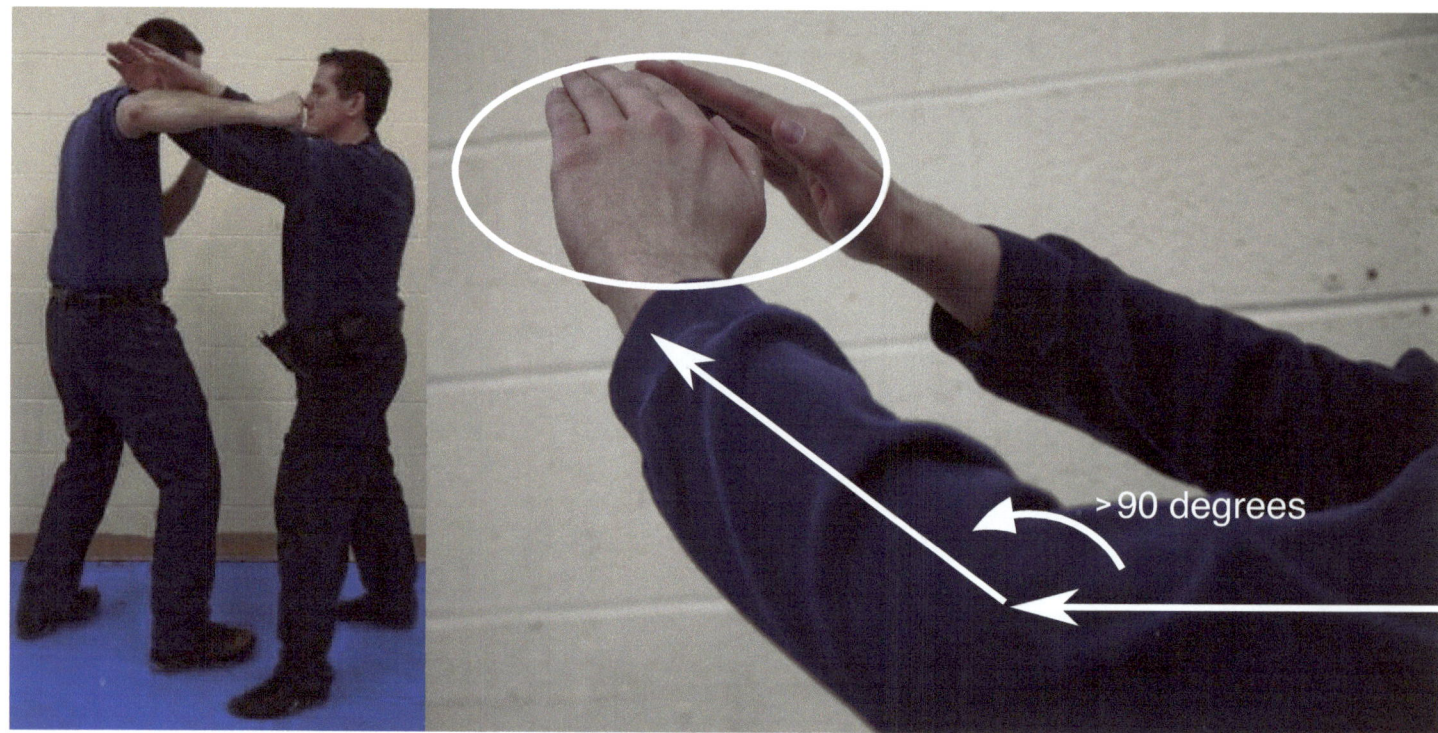

- Contact is made with the bony ridge of the hand or forearm. Fingers are cupped together for protection and contact is made on the forearm with one hand to stop the weapon from contacting the target and high into the bicep, shoulder, or chest to stop the forward momentum of the assailant.

- Once you have effectively stopped the initial impact of the weapon the second step is to stop that weapon from being able to cycle and attack again. To do this wrap their far arm over the attacking arm, pin the attackers hand into your armpit, and wrap your fingers around the base of the triceps digging into the bony protrusions where the radius and ulna connect to the humorous.

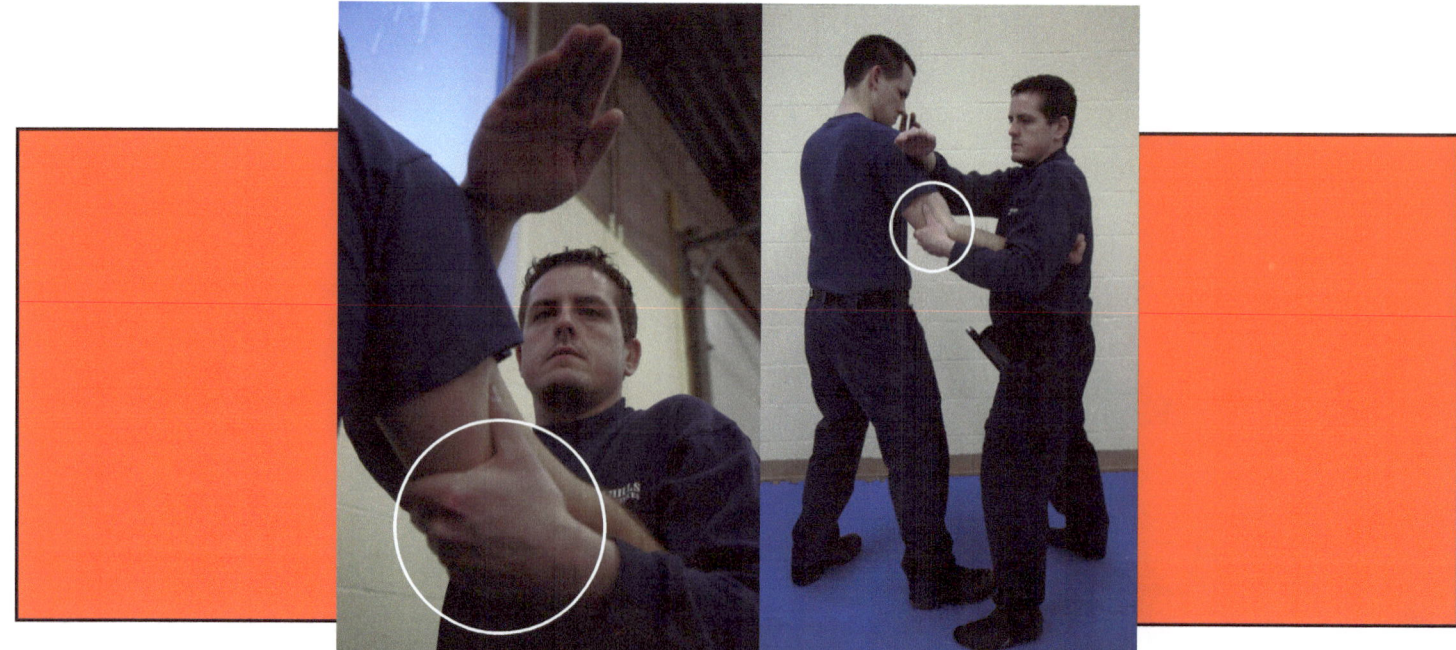

- Once the assailants arm is effectively wrapped and controlled facilitation and thought interruption strikes are encouraged. The best options are either a forearm strike to the side of the neck or a hammer fist strike to the side of the jaw. In a lethal force situation eye rakes, throat strikes or grabs, and knee strikes to the groin are all effective options.

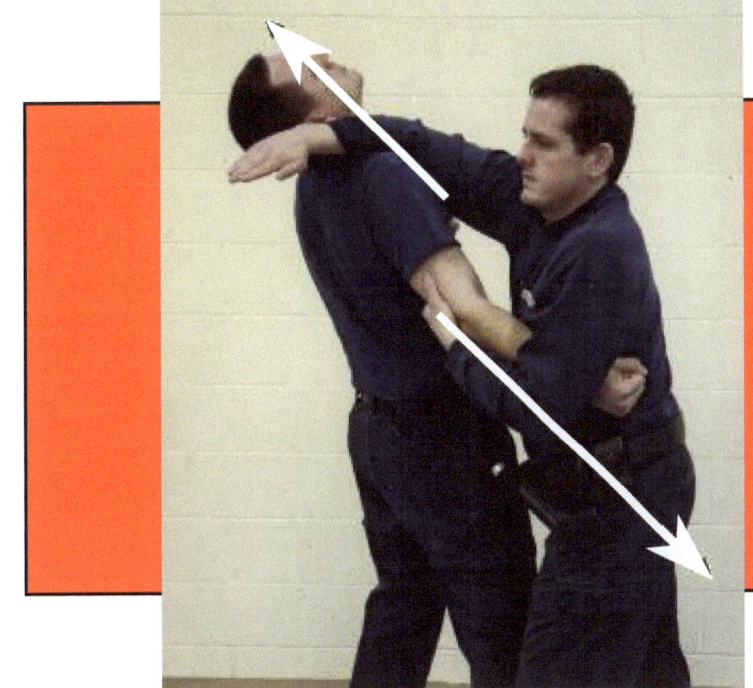

- Once control is established on the arm that attacked, your free arm applies upwards pressure into the jaw of the subject. Simultaneously draw down on the elbow with the grabbing hand and arm. This will force the subjects' eyes up and thereby break their balance to the rear. This position stops the subject from being able to effectively attack and allows you to drive in closer to the subject for the Leg Reap Takedown.

Technique #2. Leg Reap Takedown

- Once control is established and an opportunity presents itself bring your inside leg forward and behind the subject to swing it back and between the subjects legs. The term "Leg Reap" is used to illustrate that this is a violent action.

- The Reap from the leg is from the hip and takes the foot in a straight line through the subjects' center effectively kicking out one leg.

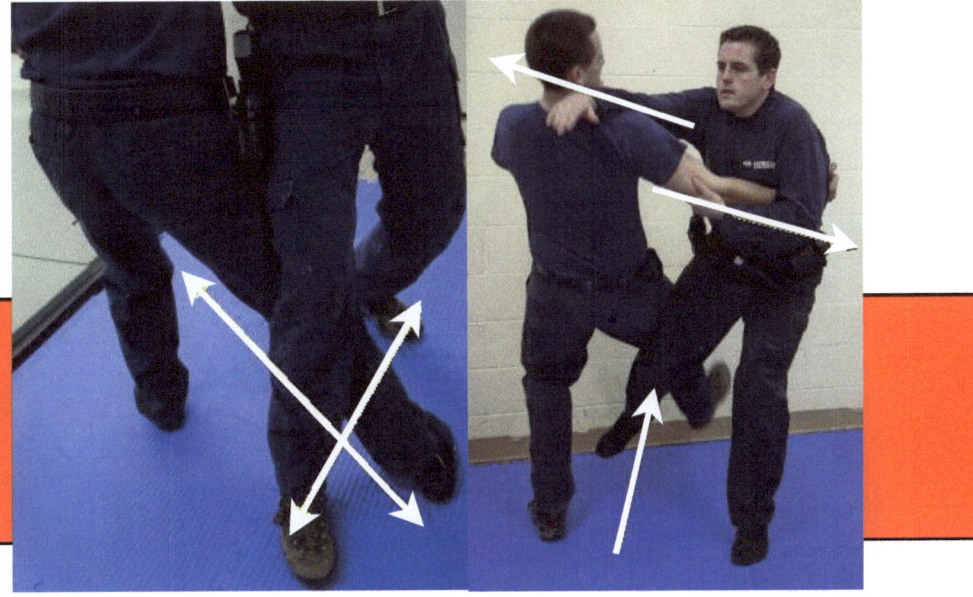

- This motion combined with the force being applied to the subjects' jaw tilting their head back takes their balance and forces them to fall to the ground.

Technique #3. Windmill Takedown

- In the case where the opponent attacks "Boxer Style" the leg corresponding with their attacking arm may be rearwards. In this case reaching for the leg reap will likely put you off balance and prolong the encounter. As with the leg reap steps 1-3 are the same. For the rearwards position however change techniques and utilize the Windmill Takedown.

- To initiate the Windmill takedown take control of the back of the subjects head and pull down instead of pushing up as in the Leg Reap. The best place to grip is at the base of the skull/top of the neck. The natural bony protrusions allow for a good grip at this location.

- The next step is to compromise the subjects' base by kicking the inside of their far knee with the flat of the foot. By pointing the toes out you are able to maximize surface area and increase their chances of affecting the target in a dynamic confrontation.

- Once the subjects balance has been compromised complete the Windmill takedown by pulling up and pushing the subjects head under on the control arm. Make sure they move out of the way or else the subject will run into their legs perhaps initiating a new attack.

Conclusion

In a violent altercation people are usually responding to a sudden attack and often don't even know the nature of the attack. While getting to an outside position offers more safety from incoming strikes it can be very difficult to acquire. People who are attacking will keep trying to align themselves to a target. In a violent assault it takes great skill and technical ability to maintain an outside position relative to an attacker.

It is therefore necessary you to become comfortable fighting from the position you're most likely to find yourself in. Developing a key set of strategies and techniques can keep you safe and allow you to control the situation accordingly.

> ### *Takedowns*
>
> *In many altercations your goal is to acquire a dominant position over the assailant. The most effective of these positional relationships is with the assailant lying on the ground on their front (Prone Position) and you standing on their feet.*
>
> *This for this reason it is critical you have an understanding of how to effectively control and disrupt an assailants balance.*

Chapter Testing Objectives

1. Demonstrate an understanding of Balance.
2. Demonstrate the different techniques for disrupting balance.

Understanding Balance.

Before practicing how to engage a subject with a takedown technique, it's important to have a conceptual understanding of their application, effects, and limitations.

Balance manipulation is a principle that relies on disrupting the natural homeostatic state between the relationship between the head, shoulders, hips, knees, and ankles. This can be accomplished two ways; one use of the limbs as levers, and two disrupting spinal alignment by attacking the core of the subject.

With both methods it is critical to understand the most likely outcome of the technique to predict when and where a subject is going fall. Both methods can be accomplished with striking or pushing energy.

In this chapter only spinal disruption techniques are examined.

Disrupting Balance

Technique #1. Horizontal Rear Jaw Control

- Jaw control is otherwise referred to as Head Manipulation or Jaw Manipulation

- Jaw control can be accomplished in several ways. Imagine that the subject sees the world calculated on two planes, a horizontal and a vertical. By manipulating the mandible (jaw) you're able to manipulate where the eyes look in relation to those 2 planes.

- A rear horizontal jaw control is performed from the ambush position behind the subject. It is often used to overcome handcuff resistance, stop a fleeing subject, or ambush a subject who's engaged with a 3rd party in front of them.

- The technique starts by extending your hands past the subjects head and clasping them together one over the other.

- Begin to pull your hands back catching the subject across the bridge of the nose and across the eyes.

- Strike down into the subjects' shoulder blades with their elbows.

- Finish the technique by flaring their elbows up and to the side while pushing down forcing the subject to land on their back. Remember "head to heels" and push straight down not back into you.

- Take into account space requirements and decide whether or not to stay still, step sideways or straight back while the subject is falling.

Technique #2. Horizontal Front Jaw Control

- A front horizontal jaw control is performed from the inside position. It is often used to overcome rear jaw control resistance, or when fighting from the inside position.

- The technique starts by clinching your hands behind the subjects head and clasping them together one over the other.

- Pull your hands forewords and down to direct the subjects eyes to the ground.

- Finishes the technique by flaring your elbows up and to the side while pushing down forcing the subject to land on their stomach. Remember "nose to toes" and push straight down not forewords into you.

- Take into account space requirements and decide whether or not to stay still, step sideways, straight down or straight back while the subject is falling.

Technique #3. Shoulder and Knee Manipulation

- If the subject is too tall for a Rear Horizontal Jaw Manipulation then the Rear Shoulder Pull with Knee Push technique can be used.

- A Rear Shoulder Pull with Knee Push is performed from the ambush position behind the subject.

- The technique starts by grabbing the subjects' shoulders at the trapezoids while simultaneously placing one foot on the back of the subjects mirror side leg with toes pointing out.

- Pull your hands back pulling the subject shoulders back while simultaneously pushing out into the subjects' knee. THIS IS NOT A KICK but rather must be a push.

- Finish the technique by flaring their elbows up and to the side while pushing down forcing the subject to land on their back. Remember "head to heels" and push straight down not back into you.

- Take into account space requirements and decide whether or not to stay still, step sideways or straight back while the subject is falling.

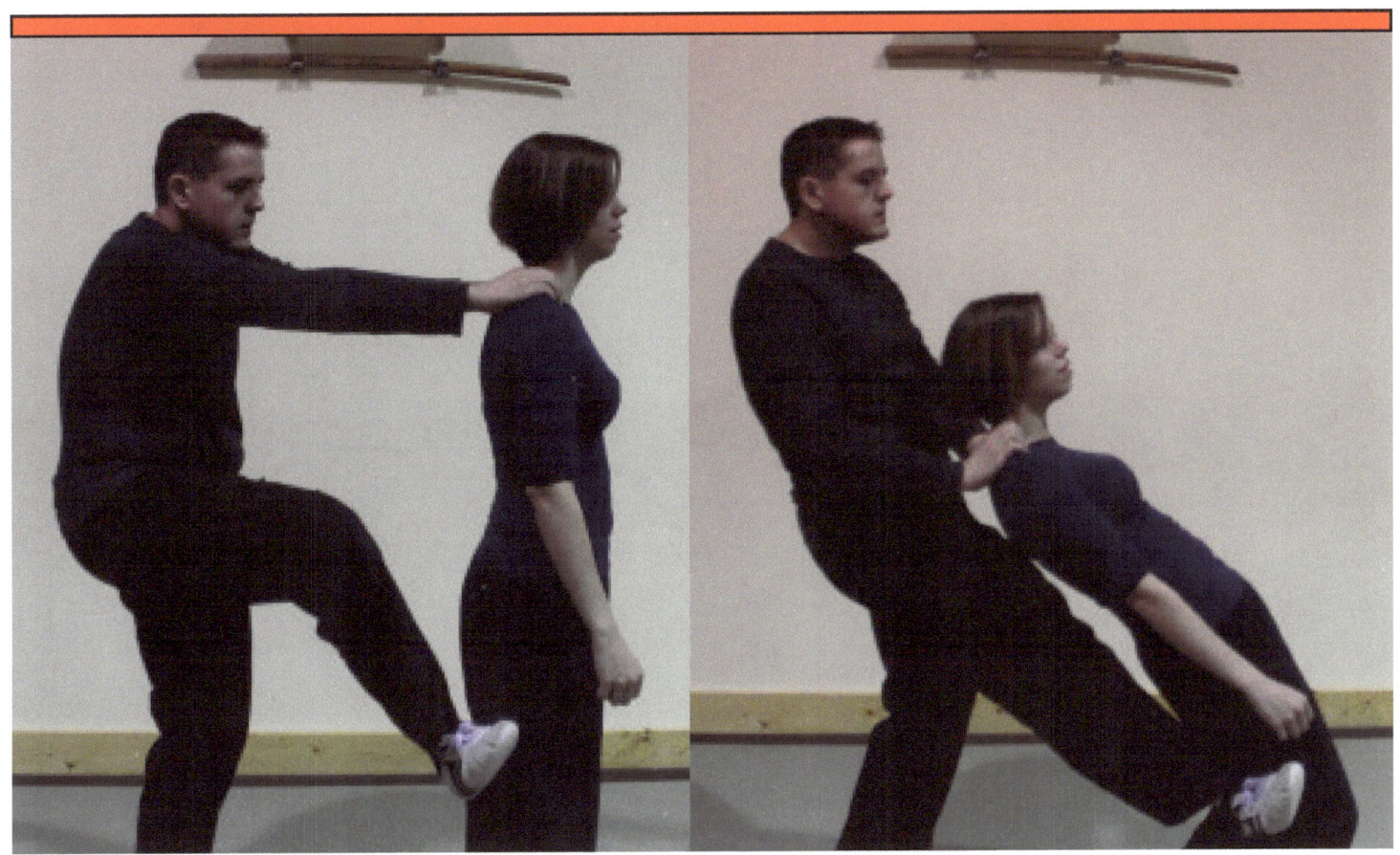

Technique #4. Breaking a rear Bear Hug

- In the event of a rear bear hug where your arms are trapped it's essential to understand what parts of your body you can still move and how to move them.

- When the assailant grabs you from behind trapping your arms against your body it's very difficult to strike them. Shin rakes, foot stomps, lifting rearwards groin kicks, and reverse head butts can all be attempted but likely won't result in loosening the assailants grip.

- When trapped in the body grab you can still move your feet, hips, and arms.

- To release the grip start by pushing down with your arms and triangulating your base by widening your feet and sliding one foot rearwards between the assailants feet.

- Next shift your hips out to the side and as you detect your assailants arms slipping upwards towards your shoulders keep lifting up with your arms with a shrugging motion in your shoulders and lifting at the elbows.

- Once the assailants arms lift over your shoulders be sure to control them with your hands so that they can't put you in a headlock.

Conclusion

The effectiveness of attempting to disrupt a subject's balance is never guaranteed. Subjects vary a great deal in terms of how well they maintain or recover balance. You should be comfortable flowing from one technique to another and executing techniques from a variety of situations and positions.

Balance Disruption techniques are generally completed as Goal #3, Finish the Fight. You must also remember there are several things to take into account before attempting to disrupt an assailants balance such as the size and apparent strength and if you have the space to move in.

> ## *Ground Fighting*
>
> *In an encounter a Ground Fight can be an extremely dangerous thing. You must understand the importance of understanding how to defend against a takedown attempt and, if the confrontation goes to the ground, understand the positions and corresponding transitions that will allow you mobility and an opportunity to fight back and protect yourself.*

Chapter Testing Objectives

1. Explain the unique factors that make ground fights so dangerous
2. Demonstrate the Sprawl and Jaw manipulation takedown defenses
3. Demonstrate the Bridge when a subject is on mount
4. Demonstrate a scissor sweep when a subject is in guard
5. Demonstrate a scissor kick reversal when a subject is on rear mount
6. Demonstrate a back door escape when a subject is on side control
7. Demonstrate Shrimping and standing sweeps
8. Demonstrate break-dancer escape when a subject has north-south position

Understanding the Ground Fight Scenario

A ground fight is seen first and foremost as a violent dangerous assault. The reasons are;

1. In a ground fight situation more kinetic energy is delivered from strikes due to the nature of stomping and kicking and the fact that counter pressure increases the transfer of kinetic energy into the target.
2. In a ground fight situation whoever maintains the top position can generate more power and use less energy by striking with gravity and body mechanics.
3. The person on the bottom position quiet often can't reach the person with the top position with strikes due to body mechanics
4. In a ground fight situation you will likely be limited as to what weapons you can access to control the subject.
5. Assailants generally become more violent once a fight hits the ground.
6. The person on the bottom position doesn't have the option of disengagement.
7. Moving on the ground requires more energy to overcome friction.
8. Your ability to deal with multiple opponents is drastically limited while on the ground.

For the reasons listed above you must train mentally and physically to treat a ground fight assault as a dangerous situation that requires immediate action. The program is broken into 3 categories; preventing the take down, defending against a standing opponent and grappling with a grounded opponent.

Technique 1. Sprawl and Matador

- As an opponent attempts a tackle shoot hips back
- Forearms simultaneously strike the opponents shoulders and press into the opponents jaw
- Push off opponent to stay standing and adjust angle to opponent
- Remember to illustrate that the primary control is from JAW CONTROL, not the actual sprawl of the hips.

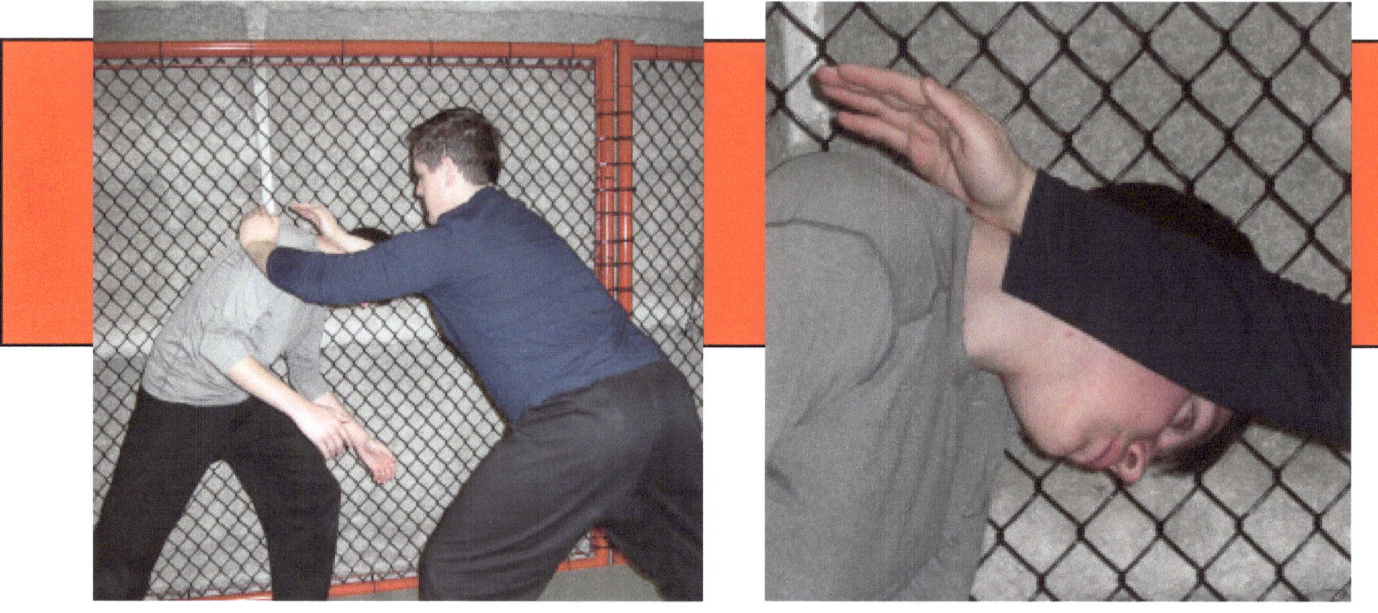

Technique #2. Sprawl to Back Control

- As opponent attempts a tackle shoot hips back
- Forearms simultaneously strike the opponents shoulders and press into the opponents jaw
- Shoot hips back
- Forearms simultaneously strike the trapezius
- "Ride" opponent to the ground and move to back mount position

Technique #3. 1 leg trap release

- From a failed sprawl the opponent might manage to wrap up 1 leg
- Strike down on back of the head with hammer fist or elbow strikes and pushes down on the back of the assailants head while dropping your body weight

- Shoot your hand down along your body and leg between your body and opponents head

- Curl your arm up over opponents face to begin jaw manipulation

- Clasp your hands together and utilizes a step and body twist to complete jaw manipulation takedown

Technique #4. Back ground fight position

- If you find yourself knocked down to the ground and your assailant is standing over you use the Back Ground Fight Position to maximize safety.

- The position is maintained by staying flat on the flat of your back with one foot tucked in close to you on the ground and the other foot raised slightly.

- From here you can use the foot on the ground to move and the other foot to kick the assailant.

- You can switch your feet depending on what direction you have to move to stay facing your assailant.

- Keep your hands and head up.

- When you deliver a low kick to your opponents' shins there's a high degree of likelihood it will bring the opponents head down to waist level. Your next kick can be a high kick to opponents face

- Various angles and targets including face, groin, shins, top of foot, and mid section can be struck.

- When the opportunity presents itself you can use a standing sweep to manipulate the assailants balance and take them down. One example is the knee bar takedown.

- To complete a knee bar takedown roll onto your side. Use your low leg to hook the back of the assailants' foot with your toes. Pull their foot towards you as you place your high foot just below their knee. With that foot push forwards to lock the opponents knee turning their leg into a lever and taking them down.

Technique #5. Shrimping

- Lift the hips to clear your body off the ground, push off the ground with the balls of the feet and simultaneously shoot hips back and reach for the feet.

- When an opponent is in your guard Shrimping can be used to create space. After creating space insert a shin and knee to create the corner and keep the subject away from you.

- Once you create space you can adopt the Back Ground Fight Position and engage with kicks.

Technique #6. Getting back to standing from the ground

- Shrimping is also used for getting up off the ground.

- After Shrimping use an arm post to establish 3 point kneeling posture.
- Be sure to keep your eyes and hands up.

- From 3 point kneeling posture standing up using a calf raise to transfer pressure from the knee to the ankle and shift your hips forwards slightly to relieve some of the pressure in the legs.

Technique #7. Bridging when subject on full mount

- If the assailant gets on your Mount it is very dangerous for you. They can use body mechanics to strike down into your head and face but you cannot effectively strike upwards at them.

- It is imperative to force the assailant to use their hands to maintain their balance instead of striking you. Grabbing their arms is ineffective because they can generate enough movement and strength to break your grip.

- Use your knee to drive straight up into the base of their spine to shift their weight forwards and force them to put their hands down on the ground.

- Once your assailants' hands are on the ground trap one of their ankles with the back of one of your legs and grab their elbow.

- To complete the bridge raise your hips off the ground as high as possible by pushing off the ground with the balls of your feet.

- Once your hips are off the ground look over one of your shoulders to set an angle and roll to that side.

- You can use jaw control to assist.

Technique #8. Scissor sweep when subject in guard

- In some instances when an assailant is in your guard it's difficult or impossible to use Shrimping to create space. In these circumstances using the legs to pull the subject deep into the guard makes it so that they can't create the space necessary to accelerate a strike. You can't hold a subject indefinitely in guard however. Particularly in the case of multiple opponents.

- To pull guard wrap the legs around the subject just above their hips and sit up to grab them. The best way to grab with the hands is on the back of the subjects head and their right elbow. Pull them into your core and hold them there to prevent being struck.

- When you detect an opening reverse the position using the Scissor Kick.

- While maintaining an elbow trap the open the guard and shrimping to get one leg flat to the ground. Use this leg to push the subjects posting leg from the knee using either the back of your leg or foot.

- Use your opposite leg to push into the assailants' ribs and rolling over your low leg.

- The technique is called the Scissor Sweep because your legs should cross each other through the assailants' body.

- When completed properly you can roll all the way over and on top of the assailants mount.

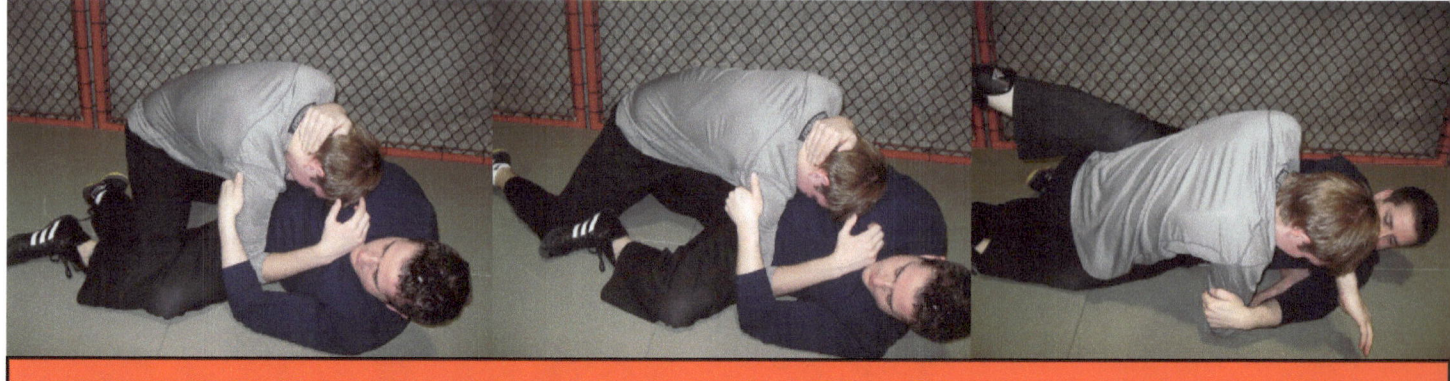

Technique #9. Scissor Kick Reversal when subject on rear mount

- The first priority when an opponent is on the Rear Mount is to protect the back of the head from strikes and the neck from a choke. This is done by shrugging the shoulders and clasping the back of the head with both hands.

- Immediately after protecting the back of the head and neck you should use the Scissor Kick Escape and scramble with jaw pressure to side control.

- This is done by digging the hips into the ground so that the subject can't wrap their legs around and hold on and violently scissor kicking the legs, one over and one under the other, to rotate the hips.

- If the subject falls onto their side then reach up and use jaw control to push their head away as they scramble to the side.

- Once side control is established you can continue to engage or escape.

- If there is space between you and the adversary during the Scissor Kick then you might roll under them and finish with the subject on your Mount. From here use the Bridge.

Technique #10. Scrambling when in Guard

- In the case of being trapped in the assailants Guard, the Guard Break can be used. First however base and control must be established. This is accomplished by using jaw control to sit back seat to heels, posture high with knees wide to control base and hands to subjects stomach

- Next walk your knee over to line up with subjects' tail bone and re establish base with other knee under subjects leg. This in combination with elbow pressure into the inner thigh and strikes will eventually open the subjects guard. Be sure to keep your other hand up to protect your head and neck.

- Once the guard is open bring the far knee over the subjects' leg to pin it to the ground and prevent them from wrapping a leg with theirs.

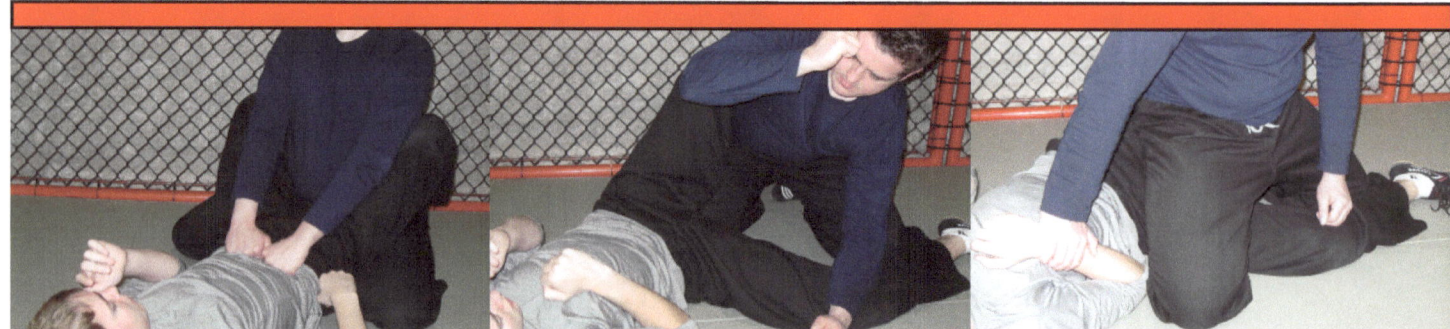

- From this position the other leg can be brought out and side control can be established. If you decide to continue to engage then the knee on belly method of getting on the mount can be used.

Technique #11. Break-dancer Reversal when in a North-South Headlock

- North-South occurs when you and the adversary are facing each other. This term can refer to many different positions in which this can happen. This is most likely to occur when both parties are on their knees and the subject either wraps your neck for a headlock or wraps around your body.

- From this position you must utilize angles. To do this first decide which side you're going to attempt to escape on. This is generally decided by which side of the opponents' body your head is pressed against.

- Once this is decided use an arm to control the assailants' hands and, in the case of a headlock, looks into the subjects ribs. Next the posture up on the far knee and arm and begins establishing their escape angle by opening their leg on the side they're going to escape to.

- Next bring the far leg through the opening they created and pressures back into the opponents' ribs with the back of your head while simultaneously sitting onto their buttock.

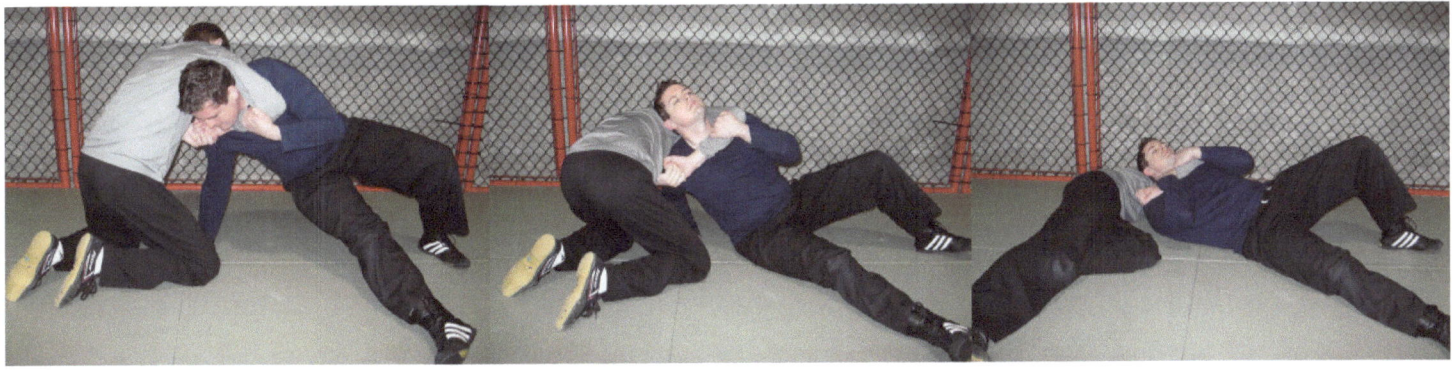

- From this position you can continue to engage by scissoring your legs and maintaining back pressure into the subject. They will either end on side control (if the opponent landed supine) or on back mount (if the assailant landed prone).

Technique #12. Back Door Escapes

- In certain situations you can't move the other person. In these situations a transition method known as "Back Door Escape" is utilized. The concept of the back door escape can be utilized from any position where the assailant is on top and you are supine.

- To utilize the Back Door Escape from a failed bridge maintain hip elevation and inserting one arm below the opponents' inner thigh.

- Use the inserted arm to create pressure over your head as hips fall back into the space and legs pull you out from under the opponent. Turn to face your adversary and adopt the Back Ground Fight Position.

Technique #13. Twisting arm control when on Mount

- Once full mount is established Twisting Arm control is the preferred method to establish a position. First use strikes for encourage your opponent to cover their head and face. Use two-on-one arm control to angle their arm across their own jaw.

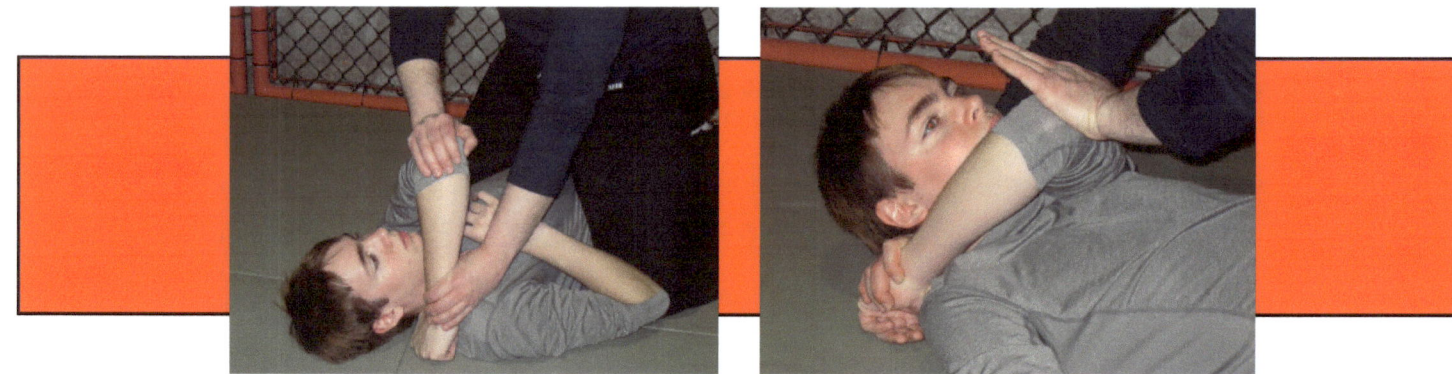

- Use body control to keep the arm in place over the jaw while reaching behind the head with one hand and grasping their wrist.

- Posture to a 3 point posture while pulling up on the subjects' wrist with arm behind their head and push down on their elbow with your other hand. Remember that power comes from the hips.

- Establish rear mount.

Conclusion

In a violent altercation you are usually responding to a sudden attack and often don't even know the nature of the attack. Ground fights are very violent and dangerous confrontations. Therefore you must be comfortable responding, moving, and transitioning on the ground.

> **Edged Weapon Defense**
>
> *Edged Weapons are a growing concern. They are nearly impossible to regulate and can take various forms, shapes and sizes. As well an assailant can cause serious injury and death with little training or skill.*
>
> *At the end of this session participants must be able to defend against an Ambush Edged Weapon attack*

Chapter Testing Objectives

1. Demonstrate and understanding of the dangers of edged weapons.

2. Demonstrate the Block, Trap, Reap technique.

Understanding Edged Weapons

Before learning how to defeat an edged weapon attack participants must first be aware of the realities of these threats.

- Edged weapons damage on a cycle where the weapon is trusted out in either a stabbing motion or a slicing motion, pulled back, and repeated.

- Interrupting the cycle is critical to surviving an assault of this nature.

- Once the cycle is interrupted tactical superiority must be established through use of a takedown.

- Knives can damage tissue on the positive (thrusting) part of a cycle or the negative (pulling back) part of a cycle.

- Knives can cause harm and damage on many angles, do not malfunction, and do not run out of ammunition.

- Because of the close contact range of a knife attack it's very easy for the assailant to hit the target.

- Because of the speed of the cycles it's very difficult to interrupt them.

- Because of arm speed it's very difficult to grab a subjects hand or wrist during an assault.

- It's rare that people will die from a single knife wound. For this reason if struck with the knife you must continue to take decisive action to protect yourself.

- The best strategy is to find cover, shielding, create space, or escape and engage with a firearm from distance.

- Because most attackers will use an ambush tactic however it's nearly impossible to access a weapon before the assailant can begin to injure you with the knife.

- Edged Weapon assaults are a lethal force threat

Technique #1. Intercepting the Cycle.

- When the subject attacks with the knife;

- Move into the subjects' power band and intercepts the attacking arm with 1 or both hands.

- Reach over the subject elbow grabbing it in a full grip and tucking it against their body. (inset)

- Next apply strikes to the subjects head and body.

This method can be used from any angle the knife travels along.

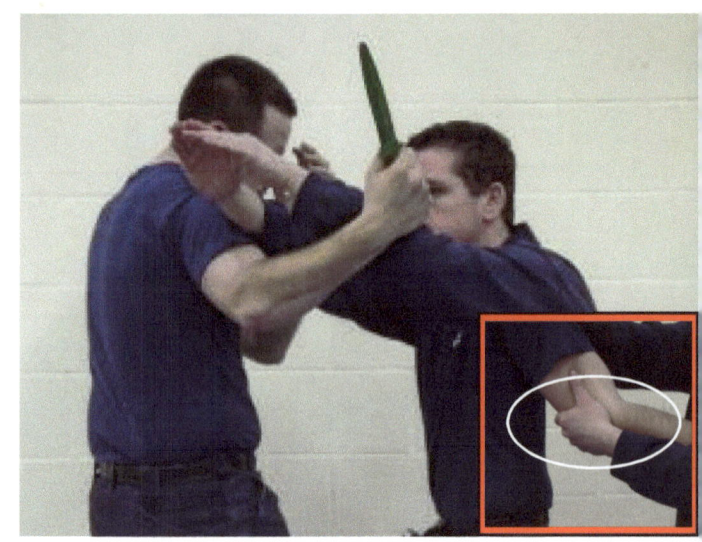

Technique #2. Leg Reap.

After you have intercepted and stopped a knife's cycle they should seek to take the subject down to the ground or if they believe their life is still in danger, and are equipped to do so, engage with contact fire with a sidearm.

Taking the subject down

- Drive past the subject while simultaneously lifting their head with a chin lift from either the hand or the elbow.

- Bring your inside leg forward and behind the subject to swing it back and between the subjects legs.

- The Reap from the leg is from the hip and takes the foot in a straight line through the subjects' center effectively kicking out one leg. This motion combined with the force being applied to the subjects' jaw tilting their head back takes their balance and forces them to fall to the ground.

Technique #3. Follow up control.

Once you have control of the subject on the ground they must decide if you're going to continue to engage and attempt to control the subject or are you going to break away, get distance, and engage with other means or escape the situation.

- Dropping into a power squat position as the subject falls and turning into them you can maintain the subjects arm position.

- Depending on the nature of the attack control strategies will change. From this position either the FTS Arm Bar Roll Over or the Wrist Twist Rollover is used to put the subject in a prone position and ½ Mount Control Handcuffing is used to secure the subject into mechanical restraints.

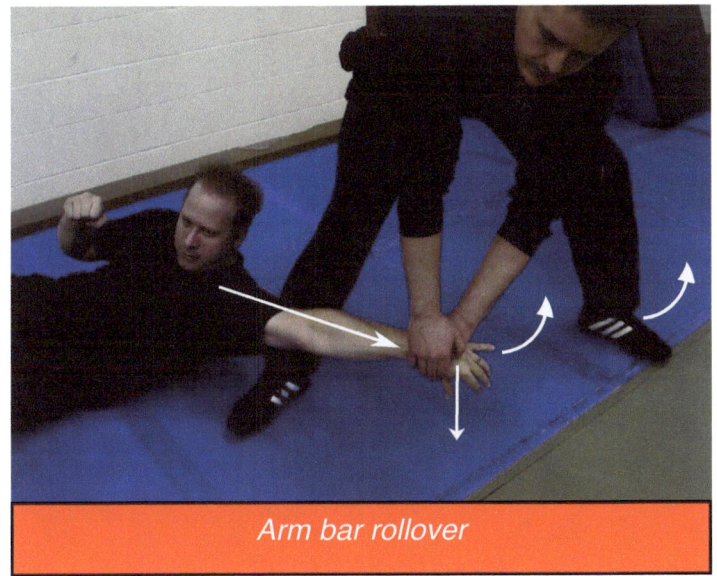
Arm bar rollover

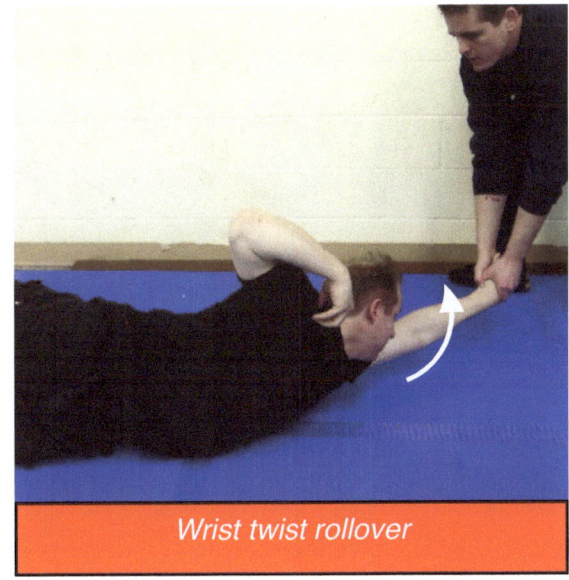
Wrist twist rollover

Conclusion

An Edged Weapon assault is one of the most serious threats you could face. It takes very little skill for the subject to be deadly with a knife but a high degree of skill for you to protect yourself in contact range. Remember priority number 1, Don't Get Hit. While it's unlikely that a single wound will kill a person it is possible. A slash or puncture to the head, face, neck, or spine could be fatal.

Because of this distance, shielding, cover, and escape should be the primary options used if threatened by a knife. If however these aren't available it is imperative that you interrupt the attack from cycling and then takes the subject down to gain a positional advantage.

> ### *First Aid/Self Aid*
>
> *An often overlooked area of physical combative training is what to do after the fight. Many instructors and students assume that after the fight everything will just sort itself out. This isn't the case.*
>
> *Your job as a trained warrior doesn't conclude once the fight is over. Likely people have been hurt and need your help, not to mention monitoring and caring for your mental health. This chapter will focus on the process immediately after a physical confrontation of First Aid and Seld Aid.*

Chapter Testing Objectives

1. Describe how to complete an emergency triage and what factors to take into account to determine whether your priority is to call for help or complete self aid/first aid.

2. Describe and Demonstrate Tactical Breathing.

3. Describe and Demonstrate methods for controlling blood loss.

4. Describe and Demonstrate methods to treating shock.

5. Describe and Demonstrate the First Aid Script.

Determining whether to call for help or begin treatment.

After a conflict that has resulted in injuries you must make a very quick decision regarding whether it's best to begin treatment first OR to call for help first. To make this decision the first piece of information you need is average response times for emergency medical services in your community. In my community an ambulance usually can arrive in 4.5min but to reach a hospital takes approximately another 15 minutes. For the purposes of this chapter these are the numbers I'm going to use to illustrate the emergency triage method. Triaging only occurs once you've reached a safe place.

Emergency Triage and Medical Treatment.

1. Primary assessment. To complete a primary assessment use the pat and look method. With both hands pat ¼ of your body feeling for wetness (blood loss), bumps or protruding bones, or pain. After you pat no more than ¼ of your body look at your hands to see if there's blood on them. Repeat until your entire body has been assessed. Do this over your entire body, even if you don't think you're hurt somewhere. Due to the physiological changes that occur during stress you might not feel an injury. This process needs to be completed quickly.

2. Time to Arrival. Once you've assessed any injuries now it's time to ask yourself, "is this injury so severe that I'll be dead by the time help gets here?" If you believe the answer is yes then start self aid BEFORE calling for help. If you think the answer is no then call for help first. That means in my community if I think I'm going to die within 4 minutes I start self aid before calling 9-1-1. The major factor when determining this is blood loss. If blood is spurting out indicating and arterial bleed, or if the amount of blood loss looks to be approximately 4 liters/1 gallon within the expected ambulance arrival time, then I need to start self aid prior to calling for help.

3. Controlling Blood Loss Using RICE. To control blood loss use RICE method. RICE stands for Rest, Ice, Compression, and Elevation. The top priority in this method for self aid is Rest and Compression. This means don't move the injured body part and put pressure directly onto the wound. If you're able to make an emergency bandage out of clothing and apply that over the wound while applying direct pressure. If the bandage becomes soaked with blood apply another one over top of the first. Do not remove the first bandage. If possible Elevate the injured body part over your heart either by lying down and raising the injured body part or by lifting it up. This may have to be done by using a prop to hold it up. If possible apply something cold to the injury also.

4. Controlling Blood Loss Using a Tourniquet. The use of a tourniquet is quit controversial. Using one might result in loss of the entire injured limb, but it might also save your life. If should be used as a last resort method for stopping blood loss. To use a tourniquet properly it is tied off above the wound but never on a joint. Belts, clothes, purse straps, just about anything can be made into a tourniquet. Once tied you can use another object such as a pen or stick to tighten it by placing the object in between your body and the tourniquet and turning the object to tighten the tourniquet. If you have a pen or something else to write with (possibly even just a finger dipped in blood) write a big T on your forehead after applying a tourniquet. This will indicate to emergency responders that you've applied one so they can look for it and remove it ASAP to save the limb it's tied off on.

5. Controlling Blood Loss Using Breath Control. Breath control can act as a reset for the Sympathetic Nervous System, which is the system that activates during a fight. As a result Heart Rate, Respiration, and Blood Pressure all decrease thereby helping to control blood loss. The breath control method follows a 4 count pattern. This means inhale for 4 seconds, hold your breath for 4 seconds, exhale for 4 seconds, hold for 4 seconds, and repeat. Generally speaking the nervous system will reset within 1 cycle, but more might be required. Breath control combined with the application of RICE or a tourniquet can greatly increase chances of survival.

6. Treating Shock. Shock can occur for several reasons. It must be treated or permanent organ damage can result. Symptoms include a weak rapid pulse, cold clammy skin, non-responsive eyes, nausea, dizziness, a feeling of faintness, and possibly a loss of consciousness. To treat shock lay the person on their back and elevate their legs. Keep them warm and treat any obvious injuries. If the person passes out roll them onto their side in case they vomit. In case you're feeling any of the symptoms follow the same procedure.

The First Aid Script

When helping another person one of your goals to is lower their heart rate, respiration, and blood pressure. This can be achieved by helping them to calm down. There is a script that can be used to help achieve this. The script can change from person to person but needs to contain 5 things.

1. Introduction. Introduce yourself and reassure the casualty that you're there to help.

2. Reassure the person that the worst is over.

3. Remind them that their body has powerful healing abilities that have already begun working for them.

4. Explain to the other person what first aid you're giving them and get them involved in the physical treatment methods as much as possible.

5. Reassure them that help is on the way and you're going to stay with them until they're being treated by professionals.

An example script might look like, "My name is Tom, and I'm here to help you. The worst is over, you're safe now. Your body has already begun healing itself and taking care of you. We're going to apply pressure to this wound, here help me pressing down right here. Help is on the way, we're going to get you to a hospital. I'll be here helping you the entire time."

Your script should be personal and flow. You need to be able to recite it during stress while you're providing first aid to another person so rehearse it frequently.

Conclusion

This chapter is not meant as a replacement for qualified instruction in first aid. You should attend a first aid class that contains adult, child, and infant CPR once per year or until you feel that you can perform those skills on a loved one when their life is at risk.

This chapter does however provide the basic process for emergency triage and treatment of blood loss and shock. It can be a difficult and scary process, especially when determining whether to treat injuries or call for help first. With training it is possible to do both simultaneously.

If you're not sure which to do always call your local emergency number (in most cases 9-1-1) and they will provide you instructions over the phone. Situations might arise however where you're unable to call for help and must take care of yourself, or others, so be prepared.

> **Crime Prevention**
>
> *Although the bulk of this textbook and the class that it supports focus' on what to do if you ever find yourself in a fight, the most powerful tool at your disposal is to understand crime and how to prevent it.*

Chapter Testing Objectives

1. Describe what is meant by "hard target" and explain what changes you can make in your personal habits, travel habits, home, and electronic presence to become a "hard target".

What is crime?

Crime is often thought of as the relationship between the offender, the victim, and the situation that brought them together. Out of the 3 variables the only one that you can control is the "victim" variable. Often we have no idea who's targeting us for a potential crime or even the situations that brought us into contact with that person.

For this reason I believe that we as individuals must take responsibility for our actions and routines and explore them for opportunities that could be exploited by potential offenders. This is not living in a state of paranoia however. Rather it's more of an evaluation of habits and routines and comparing them to common crimes and then making small changes in those routines to become a hard target.

You might not make any changes and still never be a victim of crime. You might make several changes and not be a victim of crime. It's important to recognize this because there is no way to evaluate whether or not changes to your routine have had any effect or not. From interviewing offenders however and exploring causality of crime we do know that it will decrease your chances.

Once you begin to make small changes in your life you will become switched onto a certain mindset of constant evaluation and preparedness, without paranoia. We will evaluate 4 areas of our lives and routines. They are Personal Habits, Travel Habits, Home Security, and Electronic Habits.

Personal Habits

Below are some suggestions for critical thought and evaluation regarding your Personal Habits.

Automatic Bank Tellers. When using and ATM you have your back turned to the environment and any would-be robber knows you have access to cash. For this reason accessing ATM's can be an opportunity for robbery. Whenever possible access an ATM during business hours at your own bank. If you have to use an ATM after hours for simple withdraw consider using one at an open for business service station or other business. This can limit the opportunity for robbery because the business is open and there are other people present. If this isn't an option evaluate your own bank after hours.

When conducting your evaluation you're looking for opportunities where you are alone, with your back to the environment, with opportunities for an offender to conceal themselves before an attack and escape afterwards. Things to consider are drive-thru versus walking in, and is the ATM inside the bank or outside on an exterior wall. For the most part it's more desirable to use an ATM inside a well lit building with surveillance camera's visible.

Traveling on Foot. When walking be sure to remain aware of your surroundings. This means that if wearing earphones and listening to music keep the volume down so that you can hear things around you. Also this means that your eyes will be more responsible for processing the environment so keep them up and aware. Avoid using handheld electronic devices and walking.

Be aware of high target locations and current crime trends. Walk facing traffic to decrease the chances of abduction or attack from behind. When walking around corners or other blind spots use wide angles so that you can see around the corner before travelling around it. If someone in a car wants to talk to you stay back from the car and remain vigilant. It may be a lure or distraction.

If you're walking and feel unsafe vary your routine and route and see if whoever is making you feel that way follows. If so enter a business or approach a residence. Keep a high power small flashlight on your keychain and use it in dark environments. Don't rely on personal electronic device flashlights.

When approaching your car in a parkade remain aware of blind spots and ambush locations. When approaching your car glance underneath and around it. Have your keys in your hand ready to unlock the car so that you don't have to fumble with them at the door. Glance inside the car, unlock the door, put anything inside and get in. Lock the door. Many cars automatically lock doors once the car is running or put into gear. But they don't lock the doors as soon as they close. If possible as you approach your car approach from the passenger side and walk around it and have your dominant hand free. Know where you are parked and take a direct route to the car. In high target locations use the vehicle ramp instead of stairwells and if you're feeling unsafe request a security escort to your car.

Using Public Transit. Know the schedule before you depart and limit your exposure while waiting at train stations or bus stops. While waiting stay in well lit areas or if possible in a nearby business. When on the bus or train remain awake and aware (see walking tips) with your belongings on your lap or between your feet. Prepare to exit 1 stop before your actual destination. Observe who is doing the same. Most people wait until close to the last moment not a stop or two in advance. This could be a warning sign that you're being targeted.

When Driving. Keep windows most of the way up and doors locked. Limit visibility of personal items by keeping them on the floor or in the trunk. If you're leaving your car at a service station or garage separate your keys so the only ones with the vehicle are the ignition and door keys. Shops have access to your address and can copy your house key if left there. When stopped at intersections leave enough room between your car and the one in front of you that you can maneuver and drive away if attacked. Use a locking gas cap.

When you're driving remain alert and aware. Periodically check your mirror and if you get the feeling you're being followed vary your route or stop at an open business. See if the other person continues to follow you. If you're really scared drive to a local police or fire station. If you're location has a history of fake police officers pulling people over and victimizing them and there's a police car behind you drive to the closest police station BEFORE stopping for the car. Once there co-operate with any legitimate law enforcement officers.

Be aware of high risk carjacking environments such as self service gas stations and staged breakdowns and collisions. Remain aware in these environments. If something doesn't feel right don't get out of the car. When you stop the car take a quick look around before getting out.

DO NOT give into Road Rage and ever pull over to fight another motorist. Also be aware of different security devices for your car and consider using them. Particularly if parked in public areas often or for long durations.

General Tips and Tricks. Limit the number of valuables in purses or brief cases. Have backup copies of any important documents in your car or personal carry cases. Also make sure that all the phone numbers of your banks are in your phone and know which cards you have and with which financial institution.

If you live in a high crime community consider using a 3rd party mail service with mail boxes in a secure building. Accessing mail on the street can be a high opportunity activity.

Depending on your location know and understand how to use bait wallets or money rolls and consider using a money belt or other concealable storage device. When wearing a purse or satchel keep the strap on an angle from one shoulder to the opposite hip and 1 hand resting on it. When using public restrooms remain aware of your surroundings and don't place valuables on the floor in the stall where they can be grabbed by someone on the other side.

Travel Habits

Luggage. When travelling use a business card as a luggage tag and keep it faced in so that passers-by can't read it. Use inexpensive looking hard shell luggage. Keep valuables in carry-on luggage as well as a list of everything in other luggage. When making your way through the airport or bus station keep your luggage in front of you at all times, not beside or behind you. When checking bags watch them all the way on the conveyor belt until they pass through to a secure location.

Transportation. Contact rental agencies before arriving and make arrangements. Request cars that don't have any rental agency stickers or logos on them. Purchase maps and predetermine routes before arriving at your location. Don't request them at the rental agency. If someone at the rental agency asks why you're renting the car don't give the impression you're a visitor. Lastly familiarize yourself with all features in the rental before leaving the parking lot and make sure the fuel is full.

If using taxi services book the taxi service before arriving at your destination and have it waiting for you. Don't accept a ride from anyone at the airport. Once you get into the taxi or shuttle take a picture of its credentials and text them to someone. If using public transport familiarize yourself with features, routes, schedules, and safety information before arrival.

Accommodation. Book accommodation in advance. Research locations and news for the communities they're in for current crime trends. Book rooms somewhere between the 2nd and 10th floors. Avoid ground floor and above 10th floor. Try to book rooms close to fire exits but not elevators.

Research in advance room safes and whether or not there is 24 hour staffing. Be aware that room safes are easily hacked. Do not let anyone in your room claiming to be with the hotel before checking with the front desk or calling for service. Also book your own transportation if you're not 100% sure the staff are safe and reliable.

At home. Arrange for exterior chores to be done and have interior lights on a timer to give the appearance someone's home or house-sitting. Be wary of posting updates to social media until after your return home. Also don't announce on voice mail or email auto responders that you're gone from home or for how long.

General Travel Tips. Travel with pre-paid credit cards or travellers cheques. Avoid large amounts of cash and exchange currency before departing. Let your bank know where you're travelling and the dates. Research local customs, laws, language, crimes, and infra structure before departing. Travel with a pocket translator and travel companion but keep them concealed. Avoid looking wealthy or affluent. Research emergency protocols, communication networks, and make arrangements for pre-paid cell phones etcetera before departing.

Home Security

Doors and Windows. Immediately after taking possession of a residence re-key it. Contact a local locksmith to learn about safety features in different locks. Double cylinder high security deadbolts are the most reliable. Electronic locks are prone to freezing in some climates so do your homework before purchasing one. If hiring a locksmith spend the money on a reputable one. Also make sure your door frame will support any security features on the door. I've accessed rooms and buildings before by smashing out the frame or putting a hole in the wall beside a secure door.

Make sure that front, side, or back doors have small viewers or covered windows so visitors can't see in but you can see out. Replace peep holes with wide angle viewers. Don't put pet doors in exterior doors. Garage doors don't need windows. Even in the case of attached garages ensure the door that accesses the house has separate security features than the garage door and use them. I keep a spare key for my house in a fake rock in a neighbor's yard. Don't keep one in your own yard.

Make sure windows have high quality steel locks. Examine your home from the outside during the day and night and evaluate whether or an outsider can see through window coverings. If installing bars on windows make sure the window frames can support the bars.

Equipment and Safe Room. There is some basic equipment you should have in your home. Several flashlights, candles, and fire extinguishers should be accessible from various locations in the house. One for every room is ideal. A grab bag with keys, cash, cell phone, copies of important info and ID, and clothes is also a good idea in case you have to make a hasty exit. If your bedrooms are on the second floor a rope ladder in each room is also important encase the house has to be evacuated.

If you're going to have a safe room with personal safety equipment make sure it follows any laws of jurisdiction. Make sure everyone in the house knows the location and the plan for various emergencies.

Crime Prevention Through Environmental Design. Crime Prevention Through Environmental Design (CPTED) became an important crime prevention and security strategy throughout the 1990's and continued into new millennium. The goal of CPTED is to eliminate the opportunity for crime by making the target undesirable to would be offenders.

The first thing to evaluate is lighting. Make sure the house is well lit all around the outside to eliminate locations for offenders to conceal themselves. Particularly walk ways and pathways should be well lit. Photoelectric lights that come on when the sun sets, lights on timers, or lights on motion sensors are all viable options.

The second tool is landscaping. Trees and shrubs can fennel people to certain locations or make other locations difficult and uncomfortable to access. Make sure that landscaping makes it difficult or impossible for someone to hide on your property. Tall thin shrubs and trees can accomplish this. Thorny plants under windows can deter someone from trying to access your home through those locations.

The third consideration is the use of an alarm company. Make sure you use a reputable company that offers monitoring for break-ins, glass breaks, door alarms, interior motion sensors, panic buttons, CO and CO_2 monitoring, and temperature monitoring. There are several options that even allow the owner remote access to adjust lighting and temperature in the home. Security camera's are an inexpensive option and with modern technology can be accessed remotely. Even if you're not going to invest in a security system buy some fake signage and put them on doors, windows, and gates.

A forth consideration is whether or not to get a dog. Dogs are great deterrents, particularly large breeds with a reputation for being able to hurt people. They provide an early warning system and many breeds are excellent for protecting homes and families. Dogs however require care, training, maintenance and in the case where they bite an intruder possible liability issues. Whether you have a dog or not posting signage that you do can be a great deterrent.

Finally the last habit to get into regarding home safety is how you treat unknown visitors. Women and children should never disclose that they are home alone. The door should always be checked before opening it to a stranger and any person claiming to be visiting from a professional organization should be able to produce credentials. If someone comes to your door claiming to need help offer them to wait on your front porch while you call someone for them. There's no reason for anyone to come into your home without an appointment pre-arranged by you. This includes people claiming to be emergency services. If emergency services personnel can't produce documentation or credentials be wary about letting them into your home until you can verify who they are. Obviously once you've verified their identity co-operate with any legal requests.

Electronic Security

Password protection. Use different passwords for accounts. Many people will use 1 password over and over. This is dangerous because if it's ever detected or hacked whoever discovered it will have access to all your accounts. Avoid using automatic password fillers on websites. Also periodically clear your browser history and auto fill history, or don't use them at all.

Email and Websites. Be wary of attachments and hyperlinks in email from unknown sources. Many hackers will attempt to access your personal info by sending out emails that link to what appears to be reputable websites. Often if you look at the web address however you'll see that the address doesn't match what website it's claiming to be. One way to make sure you're not being tricked into providing information on fishing sites is, if you receive an email requesting information, open a separate browser and manually enter the website address. Access your account and adjust any settings manually.

When entering information in websites make sure that they are secure. Secure websites are prefixed by "https://" but the level of security can vary. Generally speaking prefixing the address (URL) to the far left of the address bar will be an icon. Different icons indicate different levels of security and content. Educate yourself in regards to what the different icons mean for the browser that you use.

Social Media. Social Media is a hotbed for fraudulent activity on the internet. So much so that some people avoid using social media altogether. There are however several easy methods to protect yourself and still enjoy using social media websites. The first thing to understand is that most social websites automatically set new accounts to share everything you post publically. This can be changed through accessing your account settings and changing the settings for who can see your content. Often changing it so that only your contacts can see your contact is sufficient to protect your information.

You also need to be aware that as soon as you post information on social media it can be saved, downloaded, and replicated by anyone who has access to viewing it. In essence you lose control of what happens to that content as soon as it's posted so don't post anything that you want to remain in control of the distribution of.

Be wary of strangers adding you as a contact. Often one way to make sure you're sharing with only the people that you want to is to send them a message asking how you know each other. This will usually be enough to filter out frauds. Don't post all of your personal identification such as full name, date of birth, and address.

Lastly out of respect for your contacts be careful when "tagging" other people in your posts. They might be trying to protect certain aspects of their social lives and by tagging them you might be exposing what it is they're trying to protect. A simple solution is to ask people before tagging or depending on your relationship tell them after tagging them and ask them to view it and if it's not ok to let you know. If you're using social media to support a business in your business waver should be a clause letting customers know you what you post to social media and if they don't consent to it to indicate that or otherwise inform a business representative.

www.ingramcontent.com/pod-product-compliance
Lightning Source LLC
Chambersburg PA
CBHW042026150426
43198CB00002B/83